NEW-WORLD SPELLER

SECOND BOOK
For Grades Four, Five, and Six

By JULIA HELEN WOHLFARTH
Formerly Principal of Horace Mann Elementary School
Teachers College, Columbia University
Author of Self-Help Methods of Teaching English
Joint Author of Self-Help English Lessons

AND LILLIAN EMILY ROGERS
Principal of Friends' West Philadelphia School
Formerly Teacher in Horace Mann Elementary School
Teachers College, Columbia University

SECOND REVISION
ILLUSTRATED

Yonkers-on-Hudson, New York
WORLD BOOK COMPANY
2126 Prairie Avenue, Chicago

THE VOCABULARY OF NEW-WORLD SPELLER: SECOND REVISION

THE vocabulary of *New-World Speller*, edition of 1917, was based on the investigations of children's writing vocabularies made by Jones, Studley-Ware, Smith, and school officials in Boston; on the adult letter studies made by Ayres and Cook-O'Shea; on the general vocabulary studies of Ayres and Eldridge; and on several minor, but reliable, lists.

Since 1917 some important investigations have been made, notably those of Tidyman, Fernald, officials in New Orleans, Kansas City, and other places, in the children's writing vocabulary field; those of Andersen and Horn in the adult letter field; and that of Thorndike in the general vocabulary field. Astonishing as the fact may seem, the lists resulting from the later studies do not differ materially from those of the earlier studies. Their contribution to the spelling problem lies in the confirmation of the earlier findings they afford; the evidence they afford that neither children's vocabularies nor those of adults can stand alone; and the further evidence that beyond a comparatively limited number of foundation words that appear in all lists, there is a marked divergence due to the varying interests of writers.

The authors of *New-World Speller* have recently checked its vocabulary against all the lists named above, and enough others to bring the number up to twenty-eight. *With but few exceptions, the words common to a majority of the lists were found to be already in the books.*

The changes made are few in number, and naturally occur principally in the higher grades. The present books can be used in the same classes with the older edition when necessary.

Copyright 1908, 1910, 1917, 1925, by World Book Company. Copyright in Great Britain. All rights reserved. WR-NWS 2d REV: 2-34

PRINTED IN U.S.A.

ON THE TEACHING OF SPELLING

The teaching of spelling is concerned with both vocabulary and method. The words to be taught must be those which meet actual needs, and the method must be such that the spelling will be made automatic.

Introduction

The vocabulary of this book is based upon the lists published by various scientific investigators in recent years, supplemented by lists from other reliable sources. An earnest effort has been made to include all words which belong to the writing vocabulary of the average person, and to exclude all words which are rarely used, or which are so comparatively simple that they no longer present any spelling difficulty when they come into use.

But a mere word list, no matter how well selected, is not a spelling textbook. It is the function of a textbook not only to provide suitable subject matter, but also to direct the pupil's activities upon this matter in such a way that he will master it with the greatest possible economy of time and effort. It is in this sense that the *New-World Speller* is a textbook, combining a thoroughly reliable vocabulary with methods of study which result in actual power to spell.

Learning to spell involves the formation of certain habits of mind. The most important is the habit of observing correctly the printed form of words. Next in importance, and often associated with this habit, is that of hearing words correctly. Nearly all mistakes in spelling result from the failure of children in these respects. The lessons in the *New-World Speller* have been planned to aid pupils in the formation of habits of observation.

Formation of spelling habits

Effective work in spelling, as in all school subjects, depends on attention. Forced attention may accomplish something, but

To the Teacher

what is done with interest leaves the more lasting impression. The lessons, therefore, introduce great variety into the necessary drill in order to make it attractive to the children.

Directions for study

Each year's work begins with a page of directions for study. These are addressed to the pupil, and form a vital part of the book. They should be *read* and *applied*. In addition to these general directions, nearly every lesson contains special suggestions for mastering individual words. The general and the special directions together are intended to stimulate and develop the self-activity of the pupils, and will gradually train them to attack a lesson without hesitation and learn it in the most economical way.

The power to grapple with a lesson independently, however, is not instantly acquired, no matter how clear the directions for study. The teacher must be relied upon to devote a part of the recitation period to directing the forces of her pupils, until habits of study have become established.

Methods of study

Teach the children how to study and train them to use all the helps provided in the book. They must learn to select from each lesson the words which they are sure they can spell and to give all their time and attention to the others; they must learn to sift the easy from the more difficult words and to give each group its due amount of time and attention; they must learn how to get the meaning and use of unfamiliar words; they must learn to clinch knowledge by repetition.

The greatest possible variety in presentation and drill should be introduced. The lessons may sometimes be studied by looking at the words, then closing the eyes and trying to see the words with the mind's eye; sometimes by writing them on paper or on the blackboard; sometimes by spelling them aloud; sometimes by building them with cardboard letters; sometimes by playing simple games, which may or may not take the form of a contest. Attention should be directed to the difficult combinations of letters by underlining them, by writing them with crayon or pencil of a different color, by repeating them orally many times in succession, by comparing them with other words which have the same combinations. Any device that will fix the attention upon the letters which make the word difficult will be of the greatest assistance.

The method of learning new words by spelling them aloud should be carried on in school only when teacher and pupils are studying together. The results of a few minutes taken from the recitation period for the purpose of spelling aloud the hard words of the next day's lesson will repay the outlay of time a hundredfold. After habits of study have been established, spelling lessons may be assigned for home work, and the directions for study will then be invaluable.

A child does not know how to spell a word until he can do it automatically, both orally and in writing. To develop this power, review constantly. Each day the lessons of the preceding two or three days should be quickly but thoroughly reviewed; words of special difficulty should be followed up until they are thoroughly learned; and the many regular and special reviews should by no means be omitted. Here, again, variety is of the greatest importance. Each pupil may be required to keep a blank book in which he enters from day to day the words which he has misspelled. Frequent reviews of such words will correct individual errors. Another useful device is a blank book in dictionary form kept by the teacher. The words misspelled in class may be entered under their initial and reviewed by letter, the lists being copied on the blackboard for this purpose. After a little training, the pupils will be able to write the words in this dictionary of errors, and will take pride in keeping the lists as short as possible.

Review and drill

To the Teacher

Homonyms and vowel combinations

The grouping of homonyms introduces a difficulty where none exists. It is a mere incident that *there* and *their* are pronounced alike. They are spelled differently and have entirely different meanings, and if each is repeatedly used in its proper relation to other words, the child remains unconscious of the similarity of pronunciation, and consequently no confusion arises. The same is true of all homonyms. In the higher grammar grades, when the words have been fixed, no harm can result from associating them in a drill exercise.

Though the spelling of many English words is absurd, as, for instance, *eight, trough, reign, bureau, once,* these are much less troublesome than common verb forms and words containing a sound expressed by several different vowels or combinations of vowels. *Feed, read, shield, machine, receive, here,* are illustrations. Nothing but frequent oral spelling and still more frequent writing of these words in sentences or phrases will fix them in the child's mind. If the word is important, clinch it; if it is not important, do not teach it at all.

Use of sentences and phrases

The sentences and phrases are intended for dictation. The phrases afford an economical method of giving a large amount of drill on writing related words without taking time for complete sentences. Incidentally the children learn to discriminate between groups of words which express complete thoughts and those which do not. It is a good plan to read the sentence or phrase distinctly once, and then have the pupils repeat it before writing. Insist that they write without hesitation. This involves a thorough study of the lesson.

Syllabication

Learning to see the syllables of which a word is composed is one of the most important steps in learning to spell. Pupils must ultimately learn to see the syllables in undivided words. As an aid to this end, the words in this book are usually divided when they appear for the first time in the lower grades, while in

To the Teacher

the higher grades syllabication is gradually discontinued. The exercises requiring the pupils to find the short words of which longer ones are composed, those requiring them to combine short words into longer ones, and those requiring them to copy words and divide them into syllables, are all designed to cultivate the observing powers, and long use has demonstrated that such exercises are effective.

Have the pupils constantly pronounce distinctly before spelling by syllables. Since authorities differ, pronunciation may be accepted as a safe guide in a majority of cases.

Since the purpose of correcting spelling is to fix the right form in the child's mind, keep this end constantly in view. In oral spelling, have the child who made the error spell the word correctly at once. In correcting written exercises, cross out the wrong forms, and insist on their being rewritten correctly, so that finally only correctly spelled words shall be before the pupil. Many teachers make the mistake of so correcting papers that the wrongly spelled words are the more prominent. Train pupils to leave a blank space whenever doubtful of a word, and to write the word correctly after the papers have been returned to them, underlining it for thorough study. *Correction of errors*

The dictionary habit is an invaluable one; its importance cannot be overestimated. This book provides for progressive dictionary work throughout, following a general plan begun in the primary grades. *Use of the dictionary*

In the first grade the pupils are taught the letters of the alphabet in their order, and hunt words in alphabetically arranged lists. This work is continued throughout the second and third grades. In the fourth grade exercises are introduced to show that the initial letter alone does not determine the place of a word in an alphabetical list, and pupils are taught to arrange words in true alphabetical order and to insert words into lists

To the Teacher

already prepared. After this, each grade takes an onward step until in the eighth grade the pupils will be able to use a large dictionary effectively. To accomplish this end, however, it is necessary that the work outlined be carried out as thoroughly as is the teaching of spelling. Adequate directions are given in all grades.

Adaptation to junior high schools

In the writing of this book the needs of schools organized on the junior high school plan have been kept in view. The vocabulary has been so arranged that by the end of the sixth year the large body of common words has been taught. Practically all the words most commonly misspelled have appeared, and the child who drops out of school at that point is not handicapped by finding that he has been drilled on words which he never has occasion to write, and has failed to learn the everyday words which he needs. He will, moreover, have gained sufficient power to visualize words to enable him to learn with ease new words. The child who enters the higher grades, on the other hand, will take with him a well-developed power both to study and to learn his spelling lessons promptly and effectively.

An appendix containing special spelling matter has been inserted at the end of the book. Many words required in connection with the various school subjects are more or less technical, and the time when they are needed in written work is determined by the curriculum of the subject concerned, and not by a graded spelling course. Since curricula differ, these words can be more readily located when brought together in one place than if scattered throughout the book. Provision for the use of this matter is made in special lessons.

Teacher's manual

A teacher's manual giving full and explicit directions for teaching spelling, interesting historical matter, and a bibliography for teachers, is furnished free to all teachers whose classes use these books.

FOURTH GRADE

To the Pupils of the Fourth Grade: On the following page are directions that tell you how to study your spelling lessons. Form the habit of following them whenever you study.

On page i of the Appendix, the page immediately following page 280, you will find a spelling thermometer chart that gives the spelling record of a pupil for thirty review lessons. Twenty words were dictated at each lesson. With your teacher's help, learn to read the chart, so that you will understand the story that it tells.

Make a chart for yourself and keep your spelling review record during the entire year. Your book provides for thirty-one reviews, and twenty-eight of them are written reviews. If you make twenty-eight squares from right to left, you will have just enough. If your teacher dictates twenty words for each review, your chart will have the same number of up-and-down spaces as the chart in the book. Of course you will try to beat the record that the sample chart gives.

How to Study a New Word

Read these directions every day until you have formed the habit of following them:

Make sure of the meaning of the word.
Listen carefully when you hear it pronounced.
Pronounce it very distinctly yourself.
Look at it closely. If it is not spelled just as it sounds, find the hard spot.
Spell the word aloud or softly to yourself over and over again.
Write it without the slightest hesitation.
If it is not used in a sentence in the book, make a sentence of your own for it.

How to Study a Review Lesson

Each lesson contains only a few new words. The rest are review. After you have mastered the new words, see if there are any review words that you have forgotten how to spell. If you find any, study each as if it were a new word. If the entire lesson consists of review words, do not waste time on those you know. Make a list of those you need to study. Cross out each word as it is mastered. Give special attention to the words that troubled you when you studied them for the first time.

Dictionary Lessons

Each dictionary lesson contains clear directions. Follow them carefully, and dictionary work will become a pleasure as well as a help.

Fourth Grade

1. REVIEW

This lesson and the three that follow it contain the hardest words of the second and third grades. Many of the words contain a catch. Be sure to read each day the directions for study on page 138. Make sure of all the words, and then have a spelling match.

afraid	barefoot	build	color
afternoon	beautiful	busy	coming
again	berries	can't	could
almost	birthday	carry	country
always	bottle	cheap	cousin
any	bottom	choose	cover
apron	break	church	dirty
aunt	breakfast	circle	doctor
babies	brother	circus	does

2. REVIEW

done	February	half	listen
don't	fence	having	lose
each	field	heard	making
easy	forty	horses	many
enough	friend	just	minute
every	front	knee	money
except	fruit	knock	moving
excuse	gallon	laugh	much
eyes	goose	learn	ninety
father	guess	lesson	nothing

[139]

Fourth Grade

3. REVIEW

office	ready	they	Wednesday
often	says	thirsty	week
once	second	toast	wheat
orange	shoes	tomorrow	where
paste	shovel	tonight	which
pencil	sleigh	tooth	whose
picnic	soap	Tuesday	window
pocket	some	twelve	woman
pretty	squirrel	uncle	writing
quart	stories	using	wrong
quick	sugar	vacation	wrote
quiet	sure	very	year
raise	tear	visit	yellow

4. REVIEW

the <u>blue</u> sky	<u>know</u> my lesson	<u>buy</u> some clothes
lost <u>their</u> books	bought <u>two</u> spoons	my <u>dear</u> sister
<u>meet</u> a friend	<u>threw</u> a stone	<u>through</u> the ice
<u>write</u> a letter	over <u>there</u>	a <u>pair</u> of gloves
a ripe <u>pear</u>	a rough <u>road</u>	much <u>too</u> large
<u>eight</u> dollars	<u>blew</u> away	<u>knew</u> her name
my <u>right</u> thumb	eat fresh <u>meat</u>	<u>rode</u> my pony
come <u>here</u>	<u>hear</u> the music	<u>would</u> not go

5. SPELLING MATCH

Use the words in Lessons 1, 2, 3, and 4. Help your side win.

Fourth Grade

6

Follow the directions on page 138. Do it *every day*.

"Well begun is half done."

| begin | frisk y | twist | away |
| be gin ning | crowd | apple | again |

What letter in *beginning* was doubled before adding *ing*?

7

Use each group of words in a sentence:

pane of glass	pay car fare	bread and butter
buy my ticket	enjoy the game	shall be busy
tick et	en joy	over clover

8

I could not find any mellow pears.
There were none on the tree.

| hoe | great | black | cheer |
| hoe ing | great est | blow | grade |

9

Use the last word of each column in a sentence:

love	tail	walk	east	out
dove	sail	talk	feast	shout
shove	jail	stalk	least	stout

Fourth Grade

10. DICTIONARY LESSON

If you wished to find the word *sugar* in an alphabetical list of words that contained a great many *s*'s, you would waste time if you began at the beginning of the *s* list. Instead of doing that, you notice the *second* letter, *u*, and this tells you that you must look near the end of the list. Turn to page 139. Copy all the *a* and *b* words on slips of paper. Then mix up the slips and without looking at the book arrange them in order, thinking of both the *first* and the *second* letters.

11

ti ger	el e phant	mule	monkey
bea ver	colt	sheep	bear

Which of these animals are wild? Draw a line under the two letters in *elephant* which give the sound of *f*.

12

Which animal builds its own house?
Which one has a trunk?
Does he carry his clothes in it?

east	an i mal	each
beast	cloth	peach

How many syllables has *animal*? Pronounce the word very distinctly.

Fourth Grade

13

I sew a long seam every day.
I use a needle, thread, and a thimble.

thim ble	bread	bright	beach
nee dle	thread	brother	teacher

What are the last two letters in *needle* and *thimble*?

14

What changes were made in the first word of each group to form the second and third? Spell these words aloud.

slap	fit	stir	scrub
slapped	fit ted	stirred	scrubbed
slap ping	fit ting	stir ring	scrub bing

15. REVIEW

Review Lessons 6–14. You may omit the dictionary lesson, but study the others according to the directions on page 138.

16

The farmer raises oats and other grains.

har vest	fork	spoon	close
mead ow	skate	burst	drink

Which of these words are easy because you already know how to spell *boat*, *rain*, and *head*?

Fourth Grade

17

There was a leak in the gas pipe.
The knife has a sharp edge.

| rain | cool | frost | brown |
| stain | spool | flower | goes |

In what word do you find *ea*? *dg*? *oo*? Spell *edge* aloud five times.

18

a new hair ribbon   their warm leggings
button my shoes   your pretty slippers

| rib bon | leg gings | acorn | bone |
| but ton | slip pers | across | bath |

What two words end in *on*?

19

We often use these words in school:

| rule | di vide | po em | draw |
| rul er | pu pil | after | march |

What two letters do you find in the first syllable of *divide*?

20

tool	sled	tail	tack	tin
cool	shed	sail	pack	skin
stool	abed	rail	sack	spin

[144]

Fourth Grade

21

a fresh collar   sweet honey   too large
a polite answer   a rusty knife   too sharp

po lite   hon ey   race   alike
col lar   rust y   lace   along

Which word is like *money*? What are the last two letters in *collar*?

22

What change was made in the first word of each pair before adding *ing*?

ache   be come   prom ise   in vite
ach ing   be com ing   prom is ing   in vit ing

Draw a line under the letters that make *ache* hard.

23

Each of these words may be used in speaking of a person:

tramp   nurse   own er   prince
  mas ter   teacher   clown
    doctor   Indian   Mister, Mr.

What words end in *er*? Which one ends in *or*?

24

flock   leave   boil   four   roost
block   weave   spoil   pour   roost er

[145]

Fourth Grade

25
Review Lessons 16–24.

26

There are twelve inches in a foot.
How many feet are there in a yard?
How many ounces make a pound?

ounce, oz.   foot, ft.   pound, lb.   yard, yd.   inch, in.

27

close the drawer   tie a knot   turn the knob
jerk the line   hum a tune   the other store

cute   draw er   beginning   borrow

What words have a silent letter?

28

" A bird in the hand is worth two in the bush."

build   bun dle   club   arrow
build ing   kind ness   strong   awake

29

Words we often hear at home:

couch   pi an o   porch   supper
lounge   blan kets   dinner   breakfast

Fourth Grade

30

"A stitch in time saves nine."
"Think twice before you speak."

stitch	twice	berry	pass
ditch	price	cherry	class
pitch	slice	cherries	glass

31

settle a quarrel	a birthday party		these heads
a second reader	a load of coal		can't finish

quar rel	par ty	south	begging
read er	seven	another	chase

32

float	fear	frighten	growl
trav el	sow	driving	forget

Find and spell the word which means *to put seed into the ground; to be afraid of; not to sink; to go from place to place; to make afraid.*

33

These words are formed by joining two shorter words. Study the short words, and then write the long words.

whichever	pocketbook	wheelbarrow
yourself	schoolhouse	drygoods

Copy all the words on this page beginning with *s* and arrange them in alphabetical order.

Fourth Grade

34

The monkey and the parrot live in warm countries.
The stork builds its nest on chimney tops.

country   mon keys   chim ney
coun tries   par rot   chim neys

35

Review Lessons 26–34. Be sure to read the directions on page 138.

36

hem a napkin   offer to help   a queer sight
naughty children   use a blotter   throw a snowball

plow   nap kin   naugh ty   blot ter

37

down   bread   dress   mile   root
town   spread   press   file   shoot

38

the horse's mane   plow a field   dan ger
a swarm of flies   born in February   nice ly

fod der   pitcher   spider   today

[148]

Fourth Grade

39

Coffee, ginger, and dates grow in warm countries.
Raisins are dried grapes.

| cof fee | rai sin | handle | bridge |
| gin ger | happen | heaven | follow |

Notice that both *g*'s in *ginger* have the same sound.

40

" It isn't raining rain today ; it's raining violets."

was n't   has n't   would n't

There are five contractions in this lesson. *Isn't* is the first one. Tell for what words each stands, what letter was omitted, and what takes its place. It is as much a mistake in spelling to omit the apostrophe as to omit a letter.

41

| burst a tire | raise cotton | | able to swim |
| nature study | a deep breath | | sweet honey |

| light | green | closing | gravy |
| o'clock | ground | geese | forgot |

42

able	round	flew	fire
table	pound	drew	tire
sta ble	sound	chew	wire

[149]

Fourth Grade

43

We buy vegetables of the grocer.
Potatoes are sold by the peck or bushel.

| bush | po ta to | veg e ta ble | outside |
| bush el | po ta toes | gro cer | myself |

What common word do you find in the last part of the word *vegetable*? Make sure of the rest of the word.

44

Which words are often used in school?

| o bey | whis per | necktie | ounce, oz. |
| taught | ex am ple | pound, lb. | oxen |

Be sure to pronounce the *h* in *whisper*. Pronounce it in these words also: *wheat, while, white, where.*

45

Review Lessons 36–44. Do not forget how helpful it is to spell the words aloud.

46

fore head	an kle	guess	crumb
shoul der	eye brow	sure	don't
	dinner	dipper	cream

Find the three hardest words in this lesson, and draw a line under the letters you need to study most carefully.

[150]

Fourth Grade

47. DICTIONARY LESSON

Copy the *c*, *d*, and *e* words from page 139. You will find that often there are several words having the first two letters alike, such as *cheap*, *choose*, *church*. You must then arrange them so that the *third* letters will be in the right order.

48

A crow stole a piece of cheese from a dairy.

| dair y | lion | leader | leaf |
| fair y | oatmeal | muddy | leaves |

49

A fox wanted the cheese, so he said, "Pray let me hear your lovely voice."

| want ed | scream | storm |
| love ly | scratch | track |

In which word does *c* have the sound of *s* in *sun*?

50

The proud crow tried to sing and dropped the cheese. The fox snatched it and ran quickly away.

| quick ly | thank | waves |
| qui et ly | under | wading |

[151]

Fourth Grade

51

Do you like to read about giants?

| gi ant | cave | lose | around |
| for est | moss | los ing | ashes |

What change was made in *lose* before adding *ing*?

52

What kind of work does each man named in the upper row do?

bak er	ma son	bar ber	car pen ter
miller	beans	belong	blaze
barrel	began	between	board

53

| o ri ole | swal low | robin | ostrich |
| spar row | hawk | stork | peacock |

Which words end in *ow*? Be sure to pronounce them distinctly.

54

| pepper and salt | rich soil | has been done |
| a fresh towel | play a trick | could not go |

| chain | chase | chalk | churn |

55. REVIEW

Review Lessons 46–54.

Fourth Grade

56

Dear Edward,
    Last spring father gave me a garden. I have raised onions, turnips, and other vegetables. I sell them at store prices. If you guess how much I have earned, I'll give you all the weeds I raise.
                    Your old friend,
                            Dick

| I will | tur nip | price |
| I'll | on ion | pric es |

57

| rad ish | to ma to | squash | dishes |
| pump kin | to ma toes | cab bage | grew |

  What words will be easy to learn if you remember how to spell *potato* and *potatoes*?

58. DICTIONARY LESSON

    Copy the *f, g, h, i, j,* and *k* words from page 139, and arrange them in exact alphabetical order. You will often need to notice the *third* letter of each word.

59

    Jelly is made of the juice of fruit.
    The juice is boiled in a kettle with sugar.

| ket tle | juice | floor | follow |
| plen ty | juic y | flour | drove |

Fourth Grade

60

Christmas	pres ents	member
hol i day	tur key	taking
ev er green	cran ber ries	taste

Make separate lists of the words having two and three syllables. *Holiday* formerly meant *holy day*. What change was made in *holy* before joining the words?

61

> Heap on more wood! the wind is chill;
> But let it whistle as it will,
> We'll keep our Christmas merry still.   SCOTT

whis tle	we will	chill
mer ry	we'll	chill y

Tell how *we'll* was formed from *we will*.

62

Joyful means *full of joy*. What change is made in the spelling of *full* in the following words?

joy	won der	cheer ful	de light
joy ful	won der ful	hand ful	de light ful

63

wrist	tongue	path	skirt
throat	blood	roses	sorry

What silent letter is there in *wrist*? Look out for the blunder spot in *tongue*. Read the directions for study on page 138.

Fourth Grade

64

al read y   It is already getting dark.
blos som   May is the month of apple blossoms.
mar bles   tum ble   story   straw

How many *l*'s are there in *already*? It is like *almost*.

65. REVIEW

Review Lessons 56–64.

66

among the trees   against the wall   wave a flag
toward the north   above the picture   a thick cloud

What letters do you add to *again* to form *against*?

67

Your sore finger will soon heal.
Have you suffered much?

suf fer   twig   toad   upon
lo cust   fifth   tight   wading

68

crook ed   use less   whoever   waves
fierce   pleas ant   whichever   while

Does the *i* or the *e* come first in *fierce*? Look out for the last syllable of *pleasant*.

Fourth Grade

69

My brother can swim farther than I can.
He can also run farther.

far	hol low	drift	crowd
far ther	hap pened	begun	twist

70. DICTIONARY LESSON

Copy the *s* and *t* words from Lesson 3, page 140, and arrange them in alphabetical order.

71

do an errand	blister your heel	er rand
paddle a canoe	beat a carpet	blis ter

Which syllable of *canoe* needs careful study?

72

city	lil y	lady	penny
cit ies	lil ies	la dies	pen nies

What change was made in the first word of each pair to form the second word?

73

Use the second word of each pair in a sentence:

blood	inch	out	meal	for
flood	pinch	sprout	squeal	form

Fourth Grade

74

    se vere   My cousin had a severe cough.
    quite   She seems quite well again.

why	brook	buggy	glass
enjoy	least	stalk	stout

Make a list of the words that are not spelled just as they sound. Spell each word aloud as you write it.

75. REVIEW

Review Lessons 66–74.

76

Name something which is

square	straight	bitter	cloudy
smooth	use ful	even	clear

How many *l*'s are there in *useful?* What letters in *straight* have the sound of *eigh* in *sleigh?*

77

Make long words by joining one word from the *A* list with one from the *B* list. Be sure to make real words.

A		B	
down	up	brush	card
tooth	break	set	stairs
post	eye	fast	brow

Fourth Grade

78

My waist has long sleeves.
They are trimmed with braid and velvet.

| vel vet | trim | sleeve | sign |
| river | trim ming | sleeves | reach |

79

| a broken limb | mow the grass | cost a quarter |
| correct my words | the public school | a tall grapevine |

| cor rect | quart | rompers | post office |
| pub lic | quar ter | riding | Thanksgiving |

Hunt for silent letters. Which word ends in *ic*?

80

The key of the tool chest is lost.

| hatch et | bath | key | turkey |
| lad der | lath | keys | turkeys |

What change was made in *key* and *turkey* to make them mean more than one?

81

| bri dle | puz zle | bub ble | stee ple |

| thou sand | elephant | nicely |
| animal | mule | postcard |

In what way are the words in the upper row alike? Use each of these four words in a sentence.

Fourth Grade

82

    bur y   Where did you bury the wren?
    bur ied   We buried it in the woods.

rain	stood	behind	brave
drain	backward	branch	brass

What change was made in *bury* before adding *ed*?

83

In the upper row are four pairs of words. Use the first word of each pair in asking a question and the second in answering it.

pay	build	freeze	keep
paid	built	froze	kept

clover	cookies	cork
comb	care	cracker

84

kitch en	ov en	roof	bunch
par lor	fur nace	bucket	carries

  careful   choosing   clean

What words end in *en*? What one ends in *or*? in *ace*?

85. REVIEW

Review Lessons 76–84. Make a list of the words you need to study and arrange them in alphabetical order.

Fourth Grade

MID-YEAR REVIEW

In studying Lessons 86-89, waste no time on words you already know how to spell. Give all your time to the words you are not sure of. Read page 138 and follow the directions for studying review lessons.

86. REVIEW

Review pages 139 and 140.

87. REVIEW

Review page 162.

88. REVIEW

able	bury	drawer	hatchet
above	button	edge	holiday
ache	cabbage	elephant	honey
against	canoe	errand	invite
already	cheese	example	juice
among	chilly	fairy	kettle
animal	chimney	farther	kitchen
ankle	cities	fierce	lily
beginning	coal	forehead	limb
blossom	coffee	forest	losing
breath	collar	frighten	lounge
bridle	cotton	furnace	marbles
building	cough	giant	mason
built	date	ginger	meadow
bundle	divide	grocer	mellow

Fourth Grade

89. REVIEW

merry	potato	shove	tiger
music	pour	sleeve	tomato
nature	present	sleigh	tomorrow
naughty	price	slipper	tongue
needle	promise	smooth	toward
ninety	public	spread	towel
none	pudding	square	travel
nurse	pumpkin	squash	turkey
obey	pupil	squirrel	useful
offer	puzzle	stable	vegetable
onion	quarrel	stalk	velvet
oriole	quarter	steeple	voice
oven	quietly	stitch	waist
parlor	quite	straight	weave
parrot	raisin	swarm	whisper
piano	ribbon	taught	whistle
pleasant	riding	thimble	whose
pocketbook	settle	thread	wonder
polite	severe	throat	worth
porch	shoulder	ticket	wrist

90. SPELLING MATCH

Have a spelling match, using the words reviewed in **Lessons** 86, 87, 88, and 89. Help your side win.

Fourth Grade

SPECIAL REVIEW LISTS

DAYS OF THE WEEK

Sunday Monday Tuesday Wednesday
Thursday Friday Saturday

MONTHS OF THE YEAR

January	April	July	October
February	May	August	November
March	June	September	December

NUMBERS

one	ten	nineteen	hundred
two	eleven	twenty	thousand
three	twelve	thirty	first
four	thirteen	forty	second
five	fourteen	fifty	third
six	fifteen	sixty	fourth
seven	sixteen	seventy	fifth
eight	seventeen	eighty	once
nine	eighteen	ninety	twice

ABBREVIATIONS

pint, pt.	pound, lb.	Mister, Mr.
quart, qt.	inch, in.	Mistress, Mrs
gallon, gal.	foot, ft.	Doctor, Dr.
ounce, oz.	yard, yd.	Street, St.

Fourth Grade

91

I did not make a single mistake.
There are four seasons.

sin gle	sea son	summer	winter
mis take	spring	autumn	anyway

92

Use each word in the upper row in a sentence:

o cean	coast	mist	foam	point
	candle	ladies	bull	
	carrying	also	chopped	

Look out for the blunder spot in *ocean*. Read the directions for study on page 138.

93

the basket-ball team	roller skates	roll er
keep the score	tired of being idle	i dle

asked	aching	blind	mist
anything	squeal	begged	list

94

mid dle	care	breeze	five
fid dle	dare	freeze	dive
rid dle	scare	sneeze	hive

What are the last two letters of the words in the first column? Use *dive* and *hive* in sentences.

Fourth Grade

95

The palm grows in warm countries.

| country | wil low | elm | daisy |
| coun tries | ma ple | fern | daisies |

What change was made in the word *country* to make it mean more than one?

96

ceil ing	clos et	blame	beaver
cel lar	carpet	dusty	begun
cur tain	cradle	curly	blanket

Copy all the words beginning with *c*. In which does *c* have the *s* sound? Draw a line under the first syllable of *ceiling* and the last syllable of *curtain*, and spell each aloud many times.

97

| fasten the window | do the chores | beat the rugs |
| wrap up the books | see the parade | bare feet |

| fas ten | pa rade | block | blotter |

98

| wher ev er | whit tle | pond | baker |
| scram ble | quarter | fond | barber |

Which words end in *le*?

Fourth Grade

99

Be sure to chew your food.
You must never swallow it whole.

stream	grow	ought to go
swamp	grown	feel much better

Which word has a silent letter?

100. REVIEW

Review Lessons 91–99.

101

These words are arranged in pairs. Use the first word of each pair in asking a question and the second in answering it. In which three words do you find *ought?* What one contains *aught?*

bring	think	fight	wind
brought	thought	fought	wound
win	sing	find	catch
won	sang	found	caught

102. DICTIONARY LESSON

Be very careful with these dictionary lessons. They will help you learn to use a dictionary without any trouble. None of the words in Lesson 101 are in the alphabetical list of words on pages 160 and 161. Find the exact place where each would be if it were there.

Fourth Grade

103

steam   mast
steam er   whistle
smoke   travel
cap tain   ocean

104

It was a steep climb up the mountain.
The guide said we should be dizzy.

moun tain   ear ly   crossing   dearly

In what way is *mountain* like *curtain?* Hunt for silent letters.

105

bon net   buck le   jol ly   cries
dar ling   watch   bubble   crown
     cave   born   buried

106

Breathe fresh air if you wish a healthy body.

bathe   health   mouth   club
bath   health y   place   cheerful

What are the last three letters in *bathe* and *breathe?* They have the sound of *th* in *with.*

Fourth Grade

107

The words in the upper row are often used in school:

ab sent	re cess	schol ar	re mem ber
funny	morning	means	everything

What word would the first syllable of *scholar* make if you should double the *o*? Look out for the last syllable.

108

| column of figures | ask a question | catch a hare |
| expect company | row with oars | a country lane |

| col umn | com pa ny | fork | coal |
| fig ure | ques tion | ever | colt |

109

Use the last word of each pair in a sentence:

| oar | out | rake | lunch | nest |
| roar | spout | snake | punch | vest |

110. REVIEW

Review Lessons 101–109.

111

Mother does not allow us to soil our clothes.

| al low | luck y | bush | ice |
| father | stick y | bush y | i cy |

Fourth Grade

112

Come and share my fudge.
It was given to me yesterday.

| give | yes ter day | hopped | couch |
| giv en | hammer | crooked | countries |

113

| cup and saucer | measure the potatoes | their houses |
| lie in the hammock | see the sun rise | eat beets |

| sau cer | meas ure | paste | cute |
| ham mock | rattle | rabbit | crowd |

What two letters in *saucer* have the same sound? Which comes first? Find in this lesson another word with a catch.

114

| per haps | vil lage | coun ter | seat |
| rub ber | pack age | rubbing | shore |

cranberry delight dairy

115

Use the second word of each pair in a sentence:

| please | dance | visit | take |
| tease | chance | vis it or | tak en |

116

dream of an angel	a bald man	an gel
praise my friend	sow good seed	cen ter
center of the circle	sharp lead pencil	drain

Does the *e* or the *l* come first in *angel*? Pronounce it distinctly. Look out for *center*.

117

wal nut	chest nut	beech	spruce
birch	peach	apple	pear

What silent letter do you find in *chestnut*? These words are all the names of trees.

118

lay   Please lay the book on my desk.
laid   I laid it there some time ago.
lay ing   Mother came in as I was laying it down.

Lay, laid, and *laying* are not hard to spell. Notice how they are used.

119

die	tie	dropped my tools
died	tied	pay my car fare
dy ing	ty ing	jerk the line

What change was made in *die* and *tie* before adding *ing*?

Fourth Grade

120. REVIEW

Review Lessons 111–119.

121

Do you like pork or veal better?
I don't like either. I like beef.

ei ther   can't   isn't   hasn't

What animal gives us *pork? veal? beef?* Which of these words has *ee? ea?*

122

The grocer will deliver a dozen eggs.

| de liv er | a lone | become | fear |
| dozen, doz. | a shamed | float | flood |

123

Do not forget the directions for study on page 138.

| a loaf of bread | orange peel | lem on |
| rind of a lemon | make lemonade | lem on ade |

124

put ting   rag ged   pud dle   si lent

     crawl   stamp   there's
     railroad   sign   tries

Fourth Grade

125

one half	one calf	one woman
both halves	a few calves	two women
wom en	ache	against	answer

What two letters are there in *women* that you do not find in *men*? What one letter is different in *woman* and *women*? What change was made in *half* and *calf* to make them mean more than one?

126

care ful ly	dan de li on	beginning	potatoes
fam i ly	to geth er	yourself	tomatoes
	form	froze	glass

Long words are often easier to spell than some short words. *Pronounce each syllable distinctly.*

127

leath er	eight	eight cents
feath er	sleigh	ride in a sleigh
weath er	weigh	weigh the sugar

What letters are alike in the first three words?

128. DICTIONARY LESSON

Copy on slips of paper twenty words beginning with *s*. Take the words from pages which come before this one. Mix up the slips, and then arrange the words in alphabetical order.

Fourth Grade

129

Neither father nor mother heard the noise.

| either | sweep | lawn | number |
| nei ther | speck | pansy | built |

130. REVIEW

Review Lessons 121–129.

131

| sky | fly | change | cough |
| skies | flies | chang ing | none |

straight　　　grain　　　greatest

What change was made in *sky* and *fly* before adding *es* ?

132

The stormy March is come at last,
　With wind, and cloud, and changing
　　skies;
I hear the rushing of the blast,
　That through the snowy valley flies.
　　　　　　　　BRYANT

133

Use each of these words in a sentence:

| be cause | sup pose | torn | heap |
| scat ter | swam | hand ful | juicy |

Fourth Grade

134

The cricket is an insect.
What animals travel in herds?

crick et   in sect

kept   kindness   knot   ladder

135

A gay young cricket lived near an ant.
During the summer the ant worked.
The foolish cricket did nothing but dance.

fool   women   tired   leggings
fool ish   whole   leak   lovely

136

The next winter the ant's pantry was full.
But the lazy cricket had no food.
"Poor fellow!" said the ant. "He will surely starve."

pan try   sure ly   fel low   la zy

137

One evening the cricket knocked at the ant's door.
He was hungry, and shivering with the cold.
He did not deserve help, but the kind ant fed him.

eve ning   shiv er   owner   pepper
hun gry   de serve   party   pitch

Fourth Grade

138

The thistle is purple.
Do not touch it even though it is pretty.

| this tle | master | napkin | poem |
| pur ple | monkeys | plenty | radish |

What word is like *whistle?* Hunt for silent letters.

139

Make long words by joining one word from the *A* list with one word from the *B* list.

A		B	
book	base	body	where
some	bath	ball	boat
steam	every	room	case

140. REVIEW

Review Lessons 131-139.

141

| live on a ranch | a wooden mallet | o blige |
| a sewing machine | be obliging | o blig ing |

| ma chine | lum ber | roof | slice |
| mal let | wood en | roost | spoil |

Copy the hardest words and draw a line under the letters which make them hard. Spell the words aloud as you write them.

[174]

Fourth Grade

142

show er windy
sud den kite
thun der season

"It's an ill wind that blows nobody good."

143

haven't　　　　　　hadn't　　　　　　couldn't
doesn't　　　　　　weren't　　　　　shouldn't

In what way are these words alike? What letter was omitted?

144

mel on　　　cus tard　　　pick le　　　spool
soup　　　　mus tard　　　tick le　　　sprout

　　ocean　　　　　　tired　　　　　　cellar

What two words are nearly alike? What are the last two letters in *pickle* and *tickle*?

145. DICTIONARY LESSON

The following words have the first three letters alike. Arrange them alphabetically. Of which letter must you think? *Share, shall, shawl, shade, shape, shake, shave, shame, shatter, shaggy, shabby, shack, shaft.*

Fourth Grade

146

Did you ride in a wagon or in a carriage?
The hungry wolf became very lean.

| creep | stirring | suffer | tumble |
| crept | swallow | town | tune |

147

de ny	study	hurry	cop y
de nied	stud ied	hur ries	cop ies
bury	cry	try	dry
buried	cried	tried	dries

What change was made in the first word of each pair to form the second word?

148

perfect lesson	great courage	cour age
sunny pasture	peach orchard	or chard
pas ture	turkeys	turnip	useless

Spell *courage* and *orchard* aloud as you copy them.

149

dif fer ent	mat ter	stin gy	strange
strike	wasn't	wonderful	
struck	wanted	ruler	

What are the last three letters in *different*?

Fourth Grade

150. **REVIEW**

Review Lessons 141–149.

151

blouse	cloak	coat
scarf	um brel la	shoes
o ver alls	pockets	stockings

Pronounce *umbrella* very distinctly.

152

Dear Jennie,
    Uncle Charles came home last week and brought me a pearl ring. Just think! The pearl was found in an oyster! I have shown it to a great many people, and they all think it is beautiful. I wish I could show it to you.   Truly your friend,
                Dorothy

153

sol dier	dan ger	bu gle	prince
bat tle	for ward	though	oats

    blister   blood   correct

Spell *soldier* and *danger* aloud as you copy them. What are the last two letters in *bugle*?

Fourth Grade

154

It is already an hour since I came.
I meant to go, but the trip was too dangerous.

| happy | hap pi ness | danger | enjoy |
| hap pi est | delightful | dan ger ous | eyebrow |

What change was made in happy before adding *est* and *ness*?

155

| wolf | thief | shelf | knife |
| wolves | thieves | shelves | knives |

harvest   hoeing   hollow

What change was made in the words ending in *f* or *fe* to make them mean more than one?

156

a gentle answer   a wide avenue   quite sure
a common fault   wear loose clothes   very useful

| gen tle | av e nue | I'll | whole |
| com mon | jelly | manger | women |

Find the words with a catch and master them first.

157. DICTIONARY LESSON

Make a list of ten words from this page, and show where each would belong in the alphabetical lists on pages 160 and 161. Arrange the following words in an alphabetical list: *charge, chance, chat, beat, beach, beam, bear, beans, beast, bead, beaver.*

Fourth Grade

158

dis tant   They have gone to a distant city.
com mand   It is better to obey than to command.

| will ing | try | skirt | courage |
| dur ing | spry | shirt | machine |

159

Some people used to believe in fairies.

| be lieve | paint | either | women |
| chang ing | faint | neither | since |

Does the *i* or the *e* come first in *believe*?

160. REVIEW

Review Lessons 151–159.

161

First study the short words which form the long ones:

anybody	everybody	blackberries
sometime	anywhere	somewhere
without	bookcase	muskmelon

162

| dis miss | be have | es cape | quit |
| column | question | captain | healthy |

Find and study the word which means *to get away from; to leave; to send away; to act properly.*

Fourth Grade

163

Did you bait your hook with worms?
Yes, except for the very large fish.

| un less | ceiling | curtain | angel |
| un til | cellar | closet | center |

How many *l*'s are there in *until*?

164

| easy | heav y | busy | lazy |
| ea si er | heav i er | bus i er | la zi est |

What change was made in the first word of each pair to form the second word?

165

| the wasp's sting | gain or lose | mean to go |
| the lamb's wool | a sharp spear | sew a seam |

| walnut | birch | spruce | chestnut |

Wasp's and *lamb's* are not contractions. The apostrophe and *s* show that the wasp owns the sting and the lamb owns the wool.

166

| for bid | bon fire | at tic | ashamed |
| beg gar | cin ders | alone | lemonade |

guess   sure   since

167

The pigeons were on their perch.
There were only eight in all.

pig eon	good-by	fairies
on ly	good night	baseball

168

Things we sometimes eat or drink:

mince pie	chocolate soda	pumpkin pie
chicken broth	whipped cream	tomato soup

169

curtain	sleep y	lay	pay	cloth
mountain	slow ly	laid	paid	broth
fountain	bad ly	laying	paying	froth

What new word in this lesson is easy after learning to spell *curtain* and *mountain*?

170. REVIEW

Review Lessons 161–169. The school year will soon be over. After this lesson there are four more review lessons, and then you will be ready for a spelling match. Give as much time as possible to these review lessons. Learn the words so well that you will not forget them during the summer. Read the directions for study on page 138.

Fourth Grade

171. REVIEW

This lesson and the four which follow it will be your last fourth-grade spelling lessons. Now is the time to make sure of the words which trouble you. Read page 138, and then see how promptly you can learn these lessons. Try to make every minute count. Review pages 160 and 161.

172. REVIEW

Review pages 162 and 184.

173. REVIEW

Review also page 139.

absent	breathe	closet	during
allow	brought	coast	either
alone	buckle	column	enjoy
angel	calves	common	escape
anybody	captain	company	evening
ashamed	carriage	countries	except
attic	ceiling	courage	family
avenue	cellar	curtain	fasten
baseball	center	custard	feather
bathe	chance	danger	fellow
because	change	deserve	figure
beggar	chestnut	different	forward
behave	chocolate	distant	fountain
believe	cinder	dozen	gentle

Fourth Grade

174. REVIEW

Review also page 140.

grain	mustard	remember	surely
guide	neither	saucer	tease
halves	oblige	scare	thief
hammock	ocean	scatter	thought
healthy	orchard	scholar	together
heavy	ought	scramble	touch
hungry	oyster	season	umbrella
hurried	package	shelves	valley
idle	pasture	shower	village
insect	pearl	silent	visitor
knives	people	single	wagon
leather	perfect	sneeze	walnuts
lemon	perhaps	soldier	weather
machine	pickle	soup	weigh
maple	pigeon	steam	wherever
measure	purple	stingy	wolves
mistake	question	strange	yesterday
mountain	recess	suppose	young

175. SPELLING MATCH

Have either a written or an oral spelling match. Use the words reviewed in Lessons 171–174.

Fourth Grade

SPECIAL REVIEW LISTS

In the lists below are fourth-grade words which are often misspelled, underlined words which are often wrongly used, and contractions. All need special attention.

since	truly	quite	bathe
women	tired	though	angel
whole	straight	early	used
against	tying	able	ache
believe	built	answer	meant
none	among	cough	beginning
until	laid	loose	farther
building	captain	different	measure

eat <u>beech</u> nuts
<u>built</u> its nest
<u>sow</u> onion seed
<u>heard</u> a noise
<u>seems</u> quite well
hurt my <u>heel</u>
<u>beat</u> the rugs
pay car <u>fare</u>

<u>sew</u> long <u>seams</u>
a <u>herd</u> of cattle
if <u>it's</u> raining
<u>heal</u> a sore finger
a <u>fair</u> day
go to the <u>fair</u>
play on the <u>beach</u>
eat <u>beets</u>

can't	couldn't	wasn't	there's
don't	shouldn't	weren't	I'll
isn't	hasn't	it's	we'll

FIFTH GRADE

To the Pupils of the Fifth Grade: Read carefully the directions for study on the next page, and follow them always. Give special attention to what is said about using a dictionary and a notebook. Your notebook will be your own private spelling book, because it will contain only the words that you need to master.

Read also what is said on page 137 about the spelling thermometer chart. The fifth-grade work contains the same number of written reviews as the fourth grade, and you can therefore make your chart of the same size. Do not be satisfied until your thermometer rises to the highest point. Then keep it there!

Perhaps you will enjoy forming teams of six or eight pupils, and seeing which team shows most improvement during a given time.

How to Master a New Word

Remember that the steps in mastering a word are understanding its meaning, listening carefully when it is pronounced by others, pronouncing it distinctly yourself, noting the blunder spot, spelling the word over and over again either aloud or softly to yourself, and writing it without hesitation both as a single word and in a sentence.

How to Study a Review Lesson

When studying a review lesson, select the words which need study, and proceed as if they were new. If you have not already formed habits of study, be sure to do so in the fifth grade.

Dictionary Lessons

Remember that you have spelling lessons only to help you spell when you need to write letters or have written lessons in other school subjects. It may happen that you will wish to use a word you have not learned to spell. It will then be necessary to refer to the dictionary. You have already learned to find words in short alphabetical lists. This year you will learn to use a small dictionary. If your school does not provide you with one, ask your father or mother to buy one for you. It will prove a very useful friend.

The dictionary lessons are as important as any others. Do not neglect them. If you study them faithfully you will not only *learn how to use a dictionary*, but you will *form the habit of using it*.

Use of a Notebook

Get a small blank book and use it constantly in three ways: copy into it the words you misspell in each lesson and review them every day; copy into it the words selected with the help of your teacher in special lessons; and copy into it any words which you find you need in other lessons and whose spelling you learn from the dictionary.

Fifth Grade

1. REVIEW

The words in this lesson are among the most troublesome in our language. Make sure of them now.

a dear friend	over there	hear the answer
their collars	come here	would not write
the whole orange	too much	through the glass
not half enough	last week	know the doctor

ache	cough	lose	straight
again	could	making	sugar
against	country	many	sure
always	does	meant	tear
among	done	minute	they
any	don't	none	though
beginning	early	often	tired
believe	easy	piece	tonight
blue	every	raise	truly
break	guess	read	used
built	having	ready	very
busy	heard	said	wear
buy	hour	says	where
can't	just	seems	which
choose	knew	shoes	women
color	laid	since	writing
coming	loose	some	wrote

Fifth Grade

2. REVIEW

Review the abbreviations at the foot of page iv of the Appendix at the end of the book, and the numbers on page v. These words are placed in the Appendix, not because they are not important, but because it is easier to find them when placed there than if scattered through the book. For the same reason words which you may need in written lessons in connection with other school subjects are placed in the Appendix. You will have lessons from the Appendix from time to time.

3. REVIEW

already	ceiling	edge	knives
angel	center	either	leather
animal	cheese	elephant	loaf
avenue	chocolate	evening	machine
bathe	column	except	mason
because	common	farther	measure
beggar	company	figure	middle
blossom	cotton	forehead	mountains
body	courage	fountain	nature
breathe	curtain	furnace	naughty
brought	danger	guide	oblige
building	deserve	healthy	onion
bury	different	heavy	orchard
button	divide	holiday	package
captain	doesn't	juice	people
carriage	during	kitchen	perhaps

Fifth Grade

4. REVIEW

pigeon	scholar	swallow	visitor
pleasant	season	thief	wagon
potatoes	shoulder	thought	weather
present	smooth	together	weigh
promise	soldier	tongue	whistle
question	spread	toward	wonderful
quite	square	umbrella	wrap
recess	stitch	useful	wrist
ribbon	strange	vegetable	yesterday
saucer	surely	village	young

5. SPELLING MATCH

Have a spelling match, using the words reviewed in Lessons 1–4. Copy into your notebook any words you miss.

6

The squirrel gnaws its food.
What animal has warm fleece?

wool	flax	able	pretty
wool en	cotton	above	beautiful

7

colt	ride	knee	rain	palm
bolt	pride	kneel	sprain	calm

[189]

Fifth Grade

8

"A good thing can't be cruel."
"Half a loaf is better than no bread."

| cru el | loaf | pure | girl |
| lovely | loaves | cure | whirl |

9

| choke | scrape | trade | spare |

autumn   absent   also
belong   allow   alone

Change the words in the upper row to the forms in *ed* and *ing*, in this way: *smile, smiled, smiling*.

10

Words which belong together but do not have a subject and a predicate form a *phrase*. Use each of the following phrases in a sentence:

foggy weather   great pleasure   bad habit
narrow stream   fertile soil   lame ankle

measure   pleas ure   fer tile   nar row

11

| claim | pre tend | attic | beast |
| steer | men tion | res cue | ashamed |

Which word means *to free from danger? to make believe? to speak of? to guide a sled or a boat? to demand as a right?*

Fifth Grade

12

"Hunger is the best sauce."

| sand wich | ba con | broth | chestnuts |
| bis cuit | hun ger | cabbage | coffee |

Draw a line under the letters which make any of these words hard, and spell the words aloud over and over again.

13

How many of these animals live in the water?

| shark | swan | tur tle | beaver |
| snail | whale | calves | lamb |

14

Use each phrase in a sentence:

wait awhile		birch tree	actor
spell aloud		nothing else	snowflakes
a while	in deed	behave	cellar
a loud	become	breath	change

15. REVIEW

Review Lessons 6–14. Consult your notebook for words you have missed. Be sure to select the words you need to study, and waste no time on the others. Read the first two paragraphs of page 186. Follow this plan in every review lesson, even though you may not be told to do so in every case.

Fifth Grade

16. DICTIONARY LESSON

In the fourth grade you learned where words belong when arranged in exact alphabetical order. You are now ready to use a dictionary.

Let us suppose that you wish to write the word *dripping*, but do not remember whether it has one *p* or two. Take your small dictionary and proceed as follows:

At the top of each page of the dictionary you will find in large letters the first word on the page and the last word. These words are called *guide words*.

Find the guide words beginning with *d*. Think where *d* comes in the alphabet and waste no time. Then find the guide words beginning with *dr*. Suppose that the first guide word on a certain page is *drawl* and the second *dropsy*. If you think of the *third* letter of *dripping* you will see that it belongs between these two guide words, and must be somewhere on that page. Look for the *dri* words. When you have found *dripping*, copy it into your notebook for review. Find the following words in your dictionary: *believe, different, minute, women, straight.*

17

Some common vegetables:

| car rot | cel er y | potato | squash |
| cu cum ber | let tuce | cranberries | pumpkin |

What is the blunder spot in *lettuce?* Find these words in your dictionary.

18

| veil | socks | fringe | leggings |
| cuff | e las tic | feather | rubbers |

Fifth Grade

19

The tower of the castle was very high.
We had a view of mountains and broad valleys.

| valley | tow er | fruit | wrong |
| valleys | cas tle | yellow | whose |

What are the last two letters in *castle?* Spell *view* aloud five times. Find *tower, castle,* and *view* in the dictionary.

20

Use in a sentence each word in the lower row:

| lock | wear | leak | lash | coop |
| shock | swear | squeak | flash | scoop |

21

It won't thaw while it is so cold.

| I am | are not | bugle | blame |
| I'm | aren't | buckle | blanket |

Won't means *will not.* It is not formed in the usual way. Tell how each of the other contractions is formed.

22. SPECIAL LESSON

With the help of your teacher make a list of the names of ten of your classmates. Begin with the names which are most common and which you may often need to write. Copy them into your notebook and learn to spell them.

Fifth Grade

23

My bicycle has good tires and a strong brake.
The frame is made of steel.

bi cy cle	brake	chimney	chew
burst	brake man	chimneys	chance

24

pol ish	shel ter	squirm	wres tle
wither	buried	covered	

Find the word which means *to dry up; to protect; to make glossy; to wriggle; to struggle with.*

25. REVIEW

Review Lessons 17–24.

26

mo las ses	ba na na	co coa	sir up
grapes	custard	muskmelon	
fudge	mustard	lemonade	

Copy the words and draw a line under the letters you need to study most.

27

real money   tender meat   fasten the door
wring clothes   pay my fare   ginger root
re al   re al ly   wring er   ten der

28

"Every cloud has a silver lining."
The lilacs are in full bloom.

| anyhow | li lac | canoe | closet |
| forever | lin ing | carpenter | bookcase |

Do you remember to read page 186 and follow the study directions?

29

In this lesson are five verbs ending in silent *e*. Change them to the forms ending in *ed* and *ing*.

plunge no tice dodge serve
 squeeze forward fountain

30. DICTIONARY LESSON

Read carefully Lesson 16, page 192. Then take your dictionary and see how quickly you can find words from this page as your teacher dictates them. Ask your teacher to time you. Try to find each word as quickly as possible.

31

Did you ever
ruin a dress? have a fever? fe ver
pack a satchel? address an envelope? en ve lope

 satch el ad dress countries
 ru in correct crooked

Fifth Grade

32

pat tern   plat ter   lan tern   awn ing
kind lings   ladder   shelves
kettle   lumber   wheelbarrow

Which two words have their last syllables alike?

33

They've done their best.

they have   <u>I have</u>   <u>we have</u>
they've   <u>you have</u>   <u>I will</u>

Write contractions for the underlined groups of words, and use each contraction in a sentence.

34

yoke of oxen   common sense   do an errand
next term   bowl of raspberries   enjoy the game

com mon   rasp ber ries   deliver   denied

35. REVIEW

Review Lessons 26–34.

36

Use in a sentence each word in the lower row:

lay   ripe   win   lift   hitch
clay   stripe   twin   gift   switch

Fifth Grade

37

"Do not look for pain and trouble;
You will find them if you do."

| troub le | speak | pain | cinders |
| doub le | spoke | pain ful | cities |

What are the last two letters in *double* and *trouble*?

38

What shorter words do you find in each long word?

butterflies	toothache	friendship
cobweb	cupboard	understand
gentleman	shoemaker	watermelon

39

| fur nish | li bra ry | laun dry | nurs er y |

dining room   porch   parlor
bathroom   kitchen   pantry

See how quickly you can find in your dictionary the words in the upper row. Pronounce *library* very distinctly.

40. SPECIAL LESSON

With the help of your teacher make a list of the names of ten of your classmates, and copy them into your notebook. Learn to spell them and review the names you learned in Lesson 22, page 193.

Fifth Grade

41

wait er   tail or   law yer   jan i tor

    law   busier   baker
    master   carefully   barber

Which words end in *er*? in *or*?

42

history   geography   language   arithmetic

    textbook   copy   dismiss
    envelope   copied   distant

Copy the words in the upper row and separate them into their syllables. Consult your dictionary to see if you are right.

43

bow and arrow   Indian wigwam   purple haze
hit the target   numb with cold   a dozen eggs

grocer   dangerous   drawer   doesn't

44

in jure   re ply   pit y   jerk
thrash   guard   hoeing   invite

Find and spell the word which means *to be sorry for; to answer; to beat soundly; to harm; to protect from danger.*

45. REVIEW

Review Lessons 36–44.

Fifth Grade

46

Dear George,
  During the vacation father took me to the Brooklyn Navy Yard. Some vessels were being fitted out for a long voyage. We went aboard one of them and it made me want to be a sailor. I wish you had been with us.

Truly your friend,
Dick

47

prob lem	ze ro	proof	frac tion
ex plain	insect	lounge	
meadow	ocean	buckle	

Find five words often used in arithmetic.

48

Change the following verbs to the forms in *ed* and *ing* in this way: *trip, tripped, tripping*. Find a silent letter.

drip	knit	strip	skim	step

49

moth	ca na ry	ea gle	os trich
quail	sparrow	turkeys	
oriole	stork	monkeys	

Copy these words and spell them aloud as you write.

Fifth Grade

50

"Enough is as good as a feast."

rough	lump	our	ear ly
enough	hump	sour	ear li er
tough	dump	scour	ear li est

51

Did you ever
use the parcel post?
send a postal card?

buy a postage stamp?
mail a money order?

| or der | post age | honey | hollow |
| post al | par cel | hungry | hurried |

52. DICTIONARY LESSON

Pronounce *insect, canary,* and *before* very distinctly. Which syllable of each word do you pronounce with more stress or force than you do the others? In the dictionary you will find the accent (') used to show which syllable is emphasized. Separate the following words into their syllables and place the accent: *beautiful, elephant, oblige, already.*

53

These words are used in business:

| busy | firm | mem′ber | price |
| busi′ness | clerk | cus′tom er | share |

What change was made in *busy* before adding *ness* to form *business?* How many syllables are there in *business?*

Fifth Grade

54

torch	el′e va tor	ri′fle	reins
ra′zor	radish	prince	
perch	raisin	pasture	

For what is each underlined word used? Which words end in *or*?

55. REVIEW

Review Lessons 46–54.

56

A line of poetry is called a verse.
Stand erect when you recite.

| po′et ry | re peat′ | drill | pray |
| re cite′ | e rect′ | single | praise |

57

Bi′ble	preach′er	hymn	choir
lately	polite	ought	
quietly	perfect	plenty	

Which of these words have to do with church? Copy *choir* and *hymn* carefully and spell them aloud as you write.

58. SPECIAL LESSON

With your teacher's help make a list of the names of your state, your city or town, and several of the most important streets. Copy the words into your notebook and learn to spell them.

Fifth Grade

59

The kernel of a nut is the part we eat.
Yeast makes bread light.

| ker′nel | voice | cra′zy | shiver |
| tim′ber | choice | silent | shower |

60

Use the first word of each group in asking a question and the second in answering it.

| swear | beat | sweep | sleep | froze |
| swore | beat′en | swept | slept | froz′en |

61

examine   discover   located   chapter
    punish   puzzle   oyster
    public   parade   quarrel

Copy all the words having more than one syllable. Separate each into syllables and place the accent where it belongs. Consult your dictionary to see if you are right.

62

Change the verbs in the upper row to the forms ending in *ed* and *ing*. Consult your dictionary to see if you are right.

hire   force   shave   e rase′   com mence′
    coal   chores   become   became

Fifth Grade

63

pare potatoes	solid gold	born in June
level spoonful	alarm clock	meet a giant
shape	gain	giant	forest

64

The cedar is an evergreen tree.

ca nal'	an'gry	shad'ow	jelly
ce'dar	be sides'	juicy	hasn't

Do not forget the steps in learning to spell a word.

65. REVIEW

Review Lessons 56–64.

66

Use in a sentence each word in the lower row:

feed	owl	ail	heat	carry
bleed	scowl	fail	cheat	marry

67

strange	passenger	person	hammock
stranger	neighbor	powder	happiest
harvest	hatchet	health	

Separate each underlined word into its syllables, and place the accent. Consult your dictionary to see if you are right.

Fifth Grade

68

" 'Tis the star-spangled banner; O long may it wave
O'er the land of the free and the home of the brave."

| it is | over | span'gled | isn't |
| 'tis | o'er | ban'ner | it's |

Notice that the contraction *o'er* is formed by combining two syllables into one instead of by combining two words.

69

| daub | roam | thresh | warn | seek |
| obey | only | losing | nobody | |

Find in the upper row the word which means *to beat grain; to look for; to wander over; to smear; to caution.*

70. SPECIAL LESSON

With the help of your teacher make a list of the states bounding your own, and the three or four most important cities of your state. Copy the names into your notebook and learn to spell them.

71

par'ent	wife	son	aunt
daugh'ter	hus'band	uncle	cousin
dairy	delightful	drew	

Pronounce these words very distinctly. Copy the five hardest words and spell each aloud five times.

Fifth Grade

72

The colt cannot get over the hedge.
The height of the hedge will prevent it.

| pre vent' | hedge | faint | dove |
| length | wedge | escape | dizzy |

73

bliz'zard	bal loon'	bar'ley	for'tune
in'ter est	fight	grown	
fierce	grain	easier	

Some of these words contain a catch. Spell the hardest words aloud.

74

daily paper	worn out	noisy children
upper book	hoarse voice	chocolate soda
smoke	snatch	steeple	sticky

75. REVIEW

Review Lessons 66–74.

76

| rav'el | sprin'kle | stock | sudden |
| scam'per | wrin'kle | ug'ly | stormy |

Consult your dictionary for the meaning of any word you do not know. What words end in *le*? What one ends in *el*?

[205]

Fifth Grade

77. DICTIONARY LESSON

Do not forget to consult your dictionary whenever you need to write a word you cannot spell. Separate the following review words into their syllables and place the accent. Ask your teacher to time you while you consult your dictionary to see if you are right.

vegetable   chocolate   bicycle   arithmetic

78

Do not waste your time or your money.
Be sure to prove your examples.

| sad′dle | gath′er | stable |
| ex change′ | squeal | suppose |

79

purse   har′ness   hal′ter   en′gine
    nick′el   swarm   swamp
    touch   towel   twice

For what is each underlined word used?

80

Use in a sentence each word in the lower row:

| rice | wire | tack | rap | camp |
| spice | tire | stack | scrap | scamp |

Fifth Grade

81

lie	Did Fido lie near the kitchen range?
lay	No, he lay near the radiator instead.
lain	He had lain there since early morning.
lying	Where is he lying now?

ra′di a tor   in stead′

Be sure to pronounce every syllable of *radiator*.

82

mo′tion   hor′rid   home′ly   e′vil

aw′ful   thread   needle
spool   thimble   sewing

83

"Look before you leap."

<u>beforehand</u>   <u>pasteboard</u>   somewhere   parrot
<u>careless</u>   <u>remember</u>   drowned   pennies

Separate each underlined word into its syllables and place the accent. Consult your dictionary to see if you are right.

84. SPECIAL LESSON

With the help of your teacher make a list of the principal trades followed in your city or town. Copy the names into your notebook and learn to spell them. Review all words in your notebook.

Fifth Grade

85

What sort of signal did you give?
The sewer drains into the river.

sew′er	ech′o	driz′zle	crowd
sig′nal	un tie′	blouse	counter

Consult your dictionary if you do not know the meaning of any of these words. Which word has a doubled letter?

86

seal a letter	plain suit of clothes	scrib′ble
scribble a note	wrench your shoulder	quite sure

riddle	pupil	piano
ruler	pepper	pickle

Which words have silent letters?

87

fearful	wonderful	willful	playful

wonder	foam	float
wonderful	flood	manger

Fearful means *full of fear*. What change in the spelling of *full* was made in the words of the upper row?

88. REVIEW

Review Lessons 76–87, except Lesson 77.

Fifth Grade

MID-YEAR REVIEW

89. REVIEW

Review page 187.

90. REVIEW

Review page 188 and Lesson 4, page 189.

91. REVIEW

Review also all words in your notebook.

address	cedar	else	instead
alarm	celery	engine	interest
angry	chapter	envelope	janitor
awful	choice	examine	kernel
awhile	clerk	exchange	laundry
bacon	cocoa	explain	lawyer
balloon	commence	fertile	leap
banana	cruel	fever	length
beaten	cucumber	fortune	lettuce
biscuit	cupboard	frozen	level
blizzard	customer	furnish	library
bowl	daughter	gentleman	loaves
broad	discover	gnaw	located
business	double	guard	mention
canal	doubtful	habit	molasses
canary	eagle	height	motion
careless	echo	hoarse	narrow
carrot	elevator	injure	neighbor

Fifth Grade

92. REVIEW

bicycle brake	mail a letter	hold the reins
church choir	severe pain	his only son
sing a hymn	pare an apple	made of steel

nickel	quail	shadow	trouble
noisy	radiator	sirup	veil
notice	range	solid	verse
ostrich	razor	sprain	vessel
parcel	really	sprinkle	view
parent	recite	squeeze	voyage
passenger	repeat	stranger	waste
pattern	reply	suit	wife
person	rifle	swear	wigwam

pity	sailor	switch	won't
pleasure	sandwich	tailor	woolen
poetry	satchel	term	worn
postage	sauce	toothache	wrestle
postal	scribble	torch	wringer
powder	sense	tough	wrinkle
punish	serve	tower	yeast
purse	sewer	trade	yoke

93. SPELLING MATCH

Have a spelling match, using all words reviewed in Lessons 89, 90, 91, and 92.

Fifth Grade

94

The camel is called the ship of the desert.
It can travel several days without water.

cam′el	sev′er al	stoop	aloud
des′ert	aboard	swift	aren't

What is a desert? How many *s*'s are there in the word?

95

des sert′	steak	beef′steak	co′co nut
prunes	lemons	tomatoes	
napkin	salt	lettuce	

What does *dessert* mean? Pronounce *desert* and *dessert* very distinctly, and notice the difference in accent. What difference is there in spelling?

96

in a moment	acre of land	fancy dress
exact answer	lose your temper	broad desert

mo′ment	tem′per	a′cre	oats
ex act′	fan′cy	idle	oars

97

she will	he will	spice	banner
she'll	he'll	watermelon	barley

Write the contraction of each of the following pronouns with *will: I, you, we, they.*

Fifth Grade

98

There are twenty-four sheets of paper in a quire.
"There is no royal road to learning."

| roy'al | rail'ing | besides | bleed |
| news | prize | Bible | bloom |

Are you reading page 186 *every day?* Be sure to do so unless you know the study directions by heart and are following them.

99

saucy answer	pale face		try to guess
rude act	simple example		don't know
sau'cy	sim'ple	cheat	horrid

In what words does *c* have the sound of *s*?

100

In what trade is each of the underlined words used? Consult your dictionary if you do not know the meaning of any word.

awl   **chis'el**   **har'row**   **trow'el**

    ghost   maple   stalk
    marbles   spruce   brakeman

101

leak	lay	seen	bitter
sneak	lay er	screen	lit'ter
south	north	battle	chill
south ern	north ern	cattle	chilly

[212]

Fifth Grade

102

<u>debt</u>   ac count′   val′ue   val′u a ble
   <u>check</u>   claim   earlier
   <u>daily</u>   cure   earliest

The underlined words are used in business. How was the word *valuable* formed from the word *value*?

103. REVIEW

Review Lessons 94–102.

104. DICTIONARY LESSON

Some time ago you learned that the accent is a great help in pronouncing a word. The dictionary also uses other pronunciation marks which you need to understand. There are twenty-six letters in the alphabet, but many more sounds. A letter often has several different sounds, and the dictionary uses certain marks to show which sound a letter has in a given word.

The letters *a, e, i, o, u* are called vowels. *Y* is a vowel when it has the same sound as *i*. Can you find anywhere a word which does not contain one or more vowels?

The vowels have many sounds. The sound which is the same as the name of the vowel, except in the case of *y*, is called the *long sound* and is marked as follows:

    cāne   bē   wrīte   hōle   ūse   trȳ

Each vowel has also a *short sound*, marked as follows:

    căt   bĕd   hĭt   lŏt   ŭp   trulў

Mark the long and short vowel sounds in the following words: *shady, bite, check, club, hot, she, try, catch, cube, hitch, both, pity.*

Fifth Grade

105

cab'in	stuff	grate	al'ley	ca'ble
firm	fleece	fraction	free	gather

Find the word which means *a narrow street; a large rope; a hut; a part of a stove.* Mark the long and short vowel sounds.

106

The underlined words refer to persons. What work does each do?

<u>butch'er</u>	<u>of'fi cer</u>	<u>plumb'er</u>	<u>den'tist</u>
judge	ought	lazy	
fringe	fought	crazy	

107

" All's well that ends well."
" An honest man's the noblest work of God."

hon'est	no ble	couldn't	die
haven't	no blest	doesn't	dying

Tell clearly how the contractions *all's* and *man's* are formed. Which word begins with a silent letter?

108

Change the verbs in the upper row to the forms in *ed* and *ing*.

ar range'	a muse'	ad vance'	ac cuse'
pre serve'	harness	history	
halter	hunger	geography	

Fifth Grade

109. SPECIAL LESSON

Review the names of the days of the week and the months of the year on page iv of the Appendix. Learn the abbreviation of each word.

110

Gold, silver, copper, and iron are metals. The rock in which they are found is called *ore*.

| cop′per | i′ron | indeed | knit |
| met′al | min′er | husband | lining |

Spell *iron* aloud five times. Mark all long and short vowel sounds.

111

The ore is put into a furnace. The great heat separates the metal from the ore. The liquid metal then settles because it is so heavy.

liq′uid   sep′a rate   mix′ture

How many syllables has *separate*? What one letter forms the second syllable?

112

travel	puzzle	cough	round
traveler	muzzle	trough	mound
wave	knee	quit	
grave	kneel	quite	

Fifth Grade

113. REVIEW

Review Lessons 105–112.

114

knuck′le	stom′ach	heart	el′bow
	freck′le	wrist	shoulder
	teeth	body	tongue

Copy these words. Draw a line under silent letters. Spell the hardest words aloud five times.

115

couple of bears	the whole earth	coup′le
bread dough	plan a concert	dough′nut
con′cert	language	carry	marry

116

The first five words may be used in speaking of persons. Make sure of both meaning and spelling.

or′phan	crip′ple	rob′ber	plunge
he′ro	cow′ard	pasteboard	polish

117

Is there a bridge across the creek?
" There's no such word as *fail*."

gold′en	re serve′	ail	hero
for give′	lantern	fail	heroes

Fifth Grade

118. DICTIONARY LESSON

In addition to the long and short sounds, each vowel except *y* has several other sounds. Notice that *a* has a different sound in each of the following words:

    gate   hat   ball   cart   care   ask   was   any

The dictionary has a mark for each sound, but it is not necessary for you to learn each one. The dictionary has a very simple plan for helping you with these sounds.

Suppose you look up the word *halter* in the dictionary. You will find it printed as follows: hal'ter (hal'tẽr). At the foot of the page you will find a list of key words which help you get the right sound of *a* and of *e*. You will find *a* in the word *all* and *ẽ* in the word *fẽrn*. With this help and the accent, you can pronounce *hal'tẽr* correctly. The best way to become familiar with these marks (called *diacritical marks*) is to refer to the key word whenever you need to do so.

With your teacher's help, select five hard words from your reading lesson and find out how to pronounce them.

119

These words are often used in school:

pri'ma ry	ex'er cise	e rase'	whisper
pen'man ship	cray'on	e ras'er	scholar

In which word does *c* have the sound of *s*?

120

silk'y	blood'y	gloom'y	lone'ly
scorch	preacher	prevent	
ravel	pretend	problem	

Fifth Grade

121

Many tons of freight lay upon the wharf.
The crew were loading it upon the steamer.

| eight | har′bor | walnuts |
| freight | whittle | taught |

122

fur′ni ture   mir′ror   bu′reau   fau′cet

quilt   willow   scrape
velvet   signal   snail

Each word in the upper row has a catch. Find and mark it.

123. REVIEW

Review Lessons 114–122.

124

How was the second word of each pair formed from the first?

happy	heavy	easy	busy
hap′pi ly	heav′i ly	eas′i ly	bus′i ly
merry	choose	make	come
mer′ri ly	choosing	making	coming

125

| shin′gle | plas′ter | base′ment | gal′ler y |
| pi az′za | rescue | ruin | scamper |

Fifth Grade

126

What short words do you find in each long word?

within	forefinger	yourselves	headache
gentlemen	tiresome	doughnut	midnight
understood	ourselves	maybe	lonesome

127

Did the valentine surprise you?
There was a streak of crimson in the sky.

val′en tine	crim′son	spoonful
sur prise′	scar′let	wither

How many *p*'s are there in *surprise*?

128

sweat	par′a sol	ostrich feather
sweat′er	hand′ker chief	large bundle
limb	mince	mistake
lilies	since	suffer

Does the *i* or the *e* come first in the last syllable of *handkerchief*?

129

Use each phrase in a sentence:

beneath the rubbish	below the line	grape arbor
beyond the river	ahead of time	large family
thief	thieves tease	starve

[219]

Fifth Grade

130

" Truth is mighty."
" A good name is rather to be chosen than great riches."

| rath'er | chos'en | swept |
| might'y | rich'es | target |

131

Use the first word of each pair in asking a question, and the second in answering it:

| choose | swell | string | forget |
| chose | swoll'en | strung | for got'ten |

132

dripping eaves   subject of the sentence
dose of medicine   piece of tender meat

separate   bureau   freight   furniture

In which words does *c* have the sound of *s*? Separate the underlined words into their syllables and consult your dictionary to see if you are right.

133. REVIEW

Review Lessons 124–132.

134

sword	ce ment'	band'age	put'ty
glue	stomach	earth
heart	tongue	couple

Fifth Grade

135

Dear Mother,

Your welcome letter came this morning, and I was glad to hear that you are no worse. I like working in the hardware store and hope to succeed. In a few years I intend to have a business of my own.

Your loving son,
Frank

136

Change the verbs ending in silent *e* to the *ed* and *ing* forms:

cause	pro mote′	im prove′	prac′tice
re duce′	dropped	ticket	
fault	given	throat	

137. SPECIAL LESSON

On page vi of the Appendix, you will find a list of words relating to arithmetic. Review those you have had, and with the help of your teacher select five others to learn.

138

search	stag′ger	re main′	dis pute′
pre pare′	turtle	wedge	
thaw	valleys	whirl	

Find and spell the word which means *to walk unsteadily; to look for; to stay; to get ready; to quarrel.*

Fifth Grade

139

ride in an automobile   have a badge
join the Boy Scouts   wear a uniform

au to mo′bile   u′ni form   wrench   wring

140

Use in a sentence each word in the upper row:

trol′ley   tun′nel   hos′pi tal   fer′ry

   ho tel′   homely   navy
   zero   member   order

141

The river basin has a gentle slope.

ba′sin   ice′berg   painful   strip
is′land   globe   raspberries   stripe

Which word has a silent letter?

142

sau′sage   per′fume   poi′son   jew′el
  sav′age   slice   stirred
  sleeve   slipper   covered

Consult your dictionary for the meaning of any unfamiliar words. What two words end in *age*?

143. REVIEW

Review Lessons 134–142.

Fifth Grade

144

| season | roof | travel | button | join |
| reason | hoof | gravel | mutton | joint |

You have already learned the first word of each pair. This will help you learn the second word. Use the new words in sentences.

145

"He's true to God who's true to man."

| he is | who is | can't | isn't |
| he's | who's | don't | it's |

Which contractions were formed from *is* and another word? from *not* and another word?

146

market   bakery   grocery   groceries

stretch   reserve   beefsteak
sweater   ahead   dessert

Separate the words in the upper row into their syllables, and consult your dictionary to see if you are right.

147

en'e my   vic'to ry   can'non   bul'let

fort   couple   since
guess   liquid   already

Use in a sentence each word in the upper row.

[223]

Fifth Grade

148

long journey	generous deed	steer a sled
into mischief	district school	spoke aloud
jour′ney	gen′er ous	stain	twist
mis′chief	dis′trict	steam	tying

Consult your dictionary for the meaning of any unfamiliar word.

149

post office, P. O.	railroad, R. R.	forenoon, A.M.
afternoon, P.M.	Captain, Capt.	Doctor, Dr.

School begins at nine A.M.   It closes at three P.M.

The abbreviations for *forenoon* and *afternoon* are sometimes written in small letters.

150

We had a heavy storm with lightning and hail.
It did a great deal of injury to the crops.

injure	light′ning	spoil
in′ju ry	yourself	weave

151

Use the last word of each column in a sentence:

whistle	loss	other	tomorrow
thistle	toss	mother	borrow
bristle	boss	smother	sorrow

Fifth Grade

152

bee′tle   don′key   buf′fa lo   cat′er pil lar
    lately   royal   business
    ghost   debt   officer

How many syllables has *caterpillar? business?*

153. REVIEW

Review Lessons 144–152. Are you remembering to copy into your notebook all the words you miss? Give special attention to these words.

154

We reached the station without further delay.
We were not tired, although the distance was great.

sta′tion   de lay′   al though′
fur′ther   dis′tance   distant

How many *l*'s are there in *although?*

155. SPECIAL LESSON

On page vii of the Appendix you will find a list of words relating to geography. Review the words you have already learned; then with your teacher's help select five others you sometimes need to write, and learn to spell them.

Fifth Grade

156

write   To whom did she write the note?
wrote   She wrote it to her niece.
writ ten   She has often written to her nephew, too.

What letters in *nephew* have the sound of *f*?

157

aisle   priest   cho'rus   or'gan
    prayer   preach   hymn
    choir   church   Bible

What words contain silent letters? Copy the hardest words and spell them aloud as you write.

158

What is the capital of your state?

cap'i tal   ar'my   pris'on   honest
pres'i dent   spy   pris'on er   noble

159

prod'ucts   cli'mate   drain'age   min'er al
   min'ing   copper   ocean
   metal   iron   river

In which school subject are these words used? Use in a sentence each word in the upper row.

Fifth Grade

160

" They're truly great who are truly good."

| liquid | medicine | automobile |
| surprise | succeed | uniform |

Write the contraction of *we* and of *you* with *are*.

161

invention   collection   composition   dictionary

examination   basin   reason
island   jewel   grocery

Separate the underlined words into syllables. If you pronounce each syllable, you will have little trouble with the spelling.

162

peb′ble	cap′ture	ap pear′	jeal′ous
ped′dle	mischief	injure
journey	generous	another

163. REVIEW

Review Lessons 154–162.

164. DICTIONARY LESSON

Mark all the vowel sounds in the following words. Use the key words in your dictionary as a help. If you have no dictionary, consult page viii of the Appendix. *School, calling, father, surely, fork, pudding, turn, look.*

Fifth Grade

165

doubt	com plain'	col lect'	bruise
haul	truth		freight
doubt'ful	forgotten		cement

Which verb in this lesson means *to gather? to murmur? to draw or drag? to distrust? to hurt with a blow?*

166

re ceive'	niece	thief	chief
believe	de ceive'	ceiling	piece

The letters *ie* or *ei* occur in each of these words. Make a list of the words in which the *e* comes first. What letter comes just before the *e* in each case?

167

slippery pavement	strong or weak	pave'ment
equal amount	quire of paper	a mount'
surprise	study	trouble	vacation

168

They did not know whether to go or stay.

wheth'er	size	weigh	worth
di rec'tion	ex'tra	weight	watch

Be sure to pronounce the *h* in *whether*. Pronounce also *which, white, wheat, where, whisper*.

Fifth Grade

169

Did you ever
see a diamond sparkle?   sharpen a lead pencil?
scald your hand?   review a lesson?

di′a mond	sharp′en	niece
spar′kle	re view′	nephew

170

On page iv of the Appendix you will find a list of holidays. Review those you already know, and learn the last three on the list.

171

Use in a sentence each phrase. Consult your dictionary for the meaning of any unfamiliar word.

read fairy tales	a natural manner	rye meal
sing the scale	a narrow ridge	too weak

      victory   son   daughter

172

rise	reply	worse	awl
ris′ing	re plied′	worst	bawl

     ne′gro   study   hope
     negroes   studies   hoping

Tell clearly how the second word of each pair was formed from the first.

Fifth Grade

173

Patient work is the secret of success.

| pa'tient | suc cess' | a gree' | delay |
| safe'ly | succeed | further | distance |

Spell each of the three hardest words aloud five times.

174

Use each phrase in a sentence:

pair of scissors warm clothing too late
source of the river pair of trousers small piece

scis'sors trou'sers camel
cloth'ing art'ist sev'er al

Which word begins with an *s*, ends with an *s*, and has two *s*'s in the middle? What is the second letter of this word?

175. REVIEW

Review Lessons 165–174. Give special attention to your notebook words. Review also the following words and their abbreviations:

inch, in.   pound, lb.   dozen, doz.
foot, ft.   pint, pt.   week, wk.
yard, yd.   quart, qt.   month, mo.
ounce, oz.   gallon, gal.   year, yr.

Fifth Grade

176. REVIEW

Review Lesson 91, page 209, and Lesson 92, page 210.

177. REVIEW

Review pages ii and iii of the Appendix. These words are more often misspelled than any others in our language. You have had them all. Give special attention to those that have troubled you in the past.

178. REVIEW

account	bureau	crew	face
advance	butcher	crimson	fancy
aisle	cable	daily	faucet
although	camel	debt	firm
amount	capital	delay	forgive
amuse	capture	dentist	forgotten
appear	cement	desert	fraction
arbor	chisel	dessert	freight
arrange	chosen	diamond	furniture
badge	climate	direction	further
bakery	clothing	double	gallery
bandage	coconut	earth	generous
beefsteak	collection	easily	geography
beetle	concert	eraser	gloomy
beneath	copper	exact	gravel
beyond	couple	examine	groceries
buffalo	coward	exercise	harbor

Fifth Grade

179. REVIEW

haul	mighty	prize	size
heart	mineral	promoted	sparkle
heat	mining	prunes	stagger
heroes	mirror	receive	state
honest	mixture	remain	stomach
hospital	niece	review	stretch
hymn	noble	rising	subject
improve	northern	royal	succeed
iron	officer	rude	surprise
island	organ	saucy	sweater
janitor	parasol	scale	swollen
jealous	pavement	scissors	sword
judge	perfume	screen	traveler
knuckle	piazza	scythe	trolley
language	plumber	search	truth
liquid	plunge	secret	tunnel
lonely	poison	sentence	valuable
maybe	practice	separate	value
medicine	preserve	several	welcome
merrily	priest	shingles	wharf
metal	prison	simple	worse

180. SPELLING MATCH

Have a spelling match, using all words reviewed in Lessons 176–179.

SIXTH GRADE

TO THE PUPILS OF THE SIXTH GRADE: When you read the directions for study on the next page, you will discover that much more is demanded of you than when you were in a lower grade. You will be expected not only to master the spelling of the words you need whenever you write, but also to do it with increasing speed. You should also be more certain whether you know a word or not, and consult the dictionary at once if you are in doubt.

Make a chart like the one on page i of the Appendix, and keep your record through the year. See pages 137 and 185. Perhaps you will enjoy planning a chart that you can use for recording the time it takes you to learn any number of words from one to ten. You will, of course, record the time only when the lesson was perfectly learned. Try it!

How to Study Spelling Lessons

In the lower grades you were taught to study a new word by learning its correct pronunciation and meaning, finding the blunder spot, spelling the word over and over again, and finally writing it without hesitation. This is still the best way for you to attack a new word, but you should be gaining speed all the time.

Do you find that you see the syllables in an undivided word more quickly than you did? Do you see the blunder spot of the word almost immediately? Can you see words with your eyes closed more easily than you did in the lower grades? If you have improved in these ways, you are growing in power. During this year, time yourself occasionally to see how quickly you can thoroughly master a hard new word.

Try the following plan when striving to learn your lessons more perfectly and at the same time more promptly:

Look at the words for a few seconds and then close the eyes. Try to see the word in your "mind's eye," and if you see it clearly, open your eyes and write it. Do not try to write it unless you are perfectly sure of the spelling. If one look is not enough, try a second look, or even a third, until you see every letter clearly. It is a good plan to begin with the shorter words and advance to longer words as you grow in power. Learning a spelling lesson will be an interesting task if you look upon it as a sort of game in which you can gain skill and speed.

The Appendix contains many useful lists. You will have regular lessons on these words from time to time, but it is a good plan to discover exactly what the Appendix contains, as you will often find it useful when you are writing lessons in the various school subjects. Make the most of every help the speller gives you and of the dictionary also.

Sixth Grade

1. REVIEW

Review pages ii and iii of the Appendix. These words are more often misspelled than any others in the language. You have had them all. If any still give you trouble, master them now.

2. REVIEW

Review the days of the week, the months of the year, and the abbreviations of weights and measures on page iv of the Appendix, and the numbers on page v of the Appendix.

3. REVIEW

The words in this lesson and the next you have had in the lower grades. Make sure of them.

afraid	breathe	courage	except
although	bruise	crumb	exchange
arrange	bureau	curtain	exercise
aunt	button	deceive	fierce
automobile	capital	dessert	fortune
banana	carriage	diamond	furnace
bathe	celery	distance	generous
beneath	chocolate	double	gentleman
bicycle	chorus	dough	healthy
birthday	circle	during	heavy
biscuit	closet	engine	honest
blossom	common	envelope	hospital
bottom	company	equal	iron

Sixth Grade

4. REVIEW

made of steel   pane of glass   quire of paper
did not steal   severe pain   church choir
their books   rain hard   hold the reins

journey   office   reason   thought
juice   onion   repeat   together
knife   package   rough   tongue
laugh   parcel   saucer   travel
lemons   parent   scholar   trouble
length   passenger   scissors   umbrella
listen   patient   shoulder   valuable
machine   pattern   sleigh   vegetable
measure   people   source   visitor

medicine   picnic   square   voyage
mischief   picture   station   weather
natural   pleasure   stomach   weigh
naughty   potatoes   strange   welcome
neighbor   practice   succeed   whistle
nephew   pretty   tailor   wrong
niece   promise   thief   yellow
notice   question   thirsty   young

5. SPELLING MATCH

Have a spelling match, using all words reviewed in Lessons 1–4. Be sure to copy into your notebook for special study any words you miss.

Sixth Grade

6

"Beautiful hands are they that do
Work that is earnest and brave and true."

| ear'nest | lov'a ble | prompt | loaf |
| grate'ful | mov'a ble | cruel | loaves |

7

Change the verbs in the upper row to the forms in *ed* and *ing*. With what letter does each verb end? Is it silent or is it pronounced? Tell clearly what changes you make.

in crease'	pro pose'	pro vide'	pro voke'
carve	spare	paid
scrape	choke	owner

8

Use each phrase in a sentence. Which word has a silent letter? Which ends in *or*?

local train   handsome woman   its horns
tennis racket   good flavor   tough meat

ten'nis   rack'et   fla'vor   hand'some

9

rinse	strain	shrink	chat'ter
both'er	fellow	fertile
fault	narrow	habit

Sixth Grade

10

Her clothes were neat and of good quality.

| absent | patient | o be′di ent | dif′fer ent |
| absence | patience | o be′di ence | dif′fer ence |

Tell clearly how the first word of each pair was changed to form the second.

11

de fend′   con sent′   at tempt′   as sist′

   pretend   dandelion   knot
   mention   interesting   key

Which word means *to make an effort? to help? to guard from injury? to agree?*

12

Use the first word of each pair in asking a question and the second in answering it:

| drive | draw | speak | throw |
| driv′en | drawn | spok′en | thrown |

    wool′ly   rescue   receive

13

crutch   cush′ion   cis′tern   fleece

   kneel   shame   gnaw
   sprain   ashamed   fallen

Sixth Grade

14

hear a horse neigh   buy a marble image
lighten the load   play truant together
flight   forehead   hunger   sauce

In what other words that you have learned does *ei* have the same sound as in *neigh*?

15. REVIEW

Review Lessons 6–14. Select carefully the words needing study, and follow the directions given on page 234.

16

" He's true to God that's true to man."
" What's in a name? "
" Howe'er it be, it seems to me
   'Tis only noble to be good."

Explain each abbreviation. Which one is a contraction of syllables rather than of two distinct words?

17

A syllable added to the beginning of a word is called a *prefix*. What prefix occurs in each word in the upper row? How does it change the meaning of the simple word?

discontented   dishonest   disagreeable   disobey

    sandwich   turtle   calves
    bacon   snail   aloud

Sixth Grade

18. DICTIONARY LESSON

Name the vowels. The remaining letters are called *consonants*. A few diacritical marks are sometimes used with consonants, but it is not important that you learn them, for, as a rule, dictionaries give the correct pronunciation of consonants by spelling the word as it sounds, as follows: aisle (īl); fraction (frăk'shun). Make sure of the correct spelling of any word you wish to pronounce properly, before looking at the pronunciation helps. Look up the following words in the dictionary and notice how the dictionary helps you pronounce them: *sign, biscuit, choir, cupboard, neighbor, stranger, patient.*

19

ac'cent	vow'el	syl'la ble	con'so nant
	elastic	fringe	veil

Copy the first four words and underline the letters needing most study.

20

"The seeds of the thistle always produce thistles."

pro duce'	scen'er y	threat	lettuce
sum'mit	shield	celery	squash

21

stew	roast	sal'ad	sar dines'
cur'rants	carrot	pumpkin	
biscuit	onion	squash	

Sixth Grade

22

It is my purpose to do thorough work.
You may depend upon me.

| pur'pose | de pend' | con tain' | view |
| thor'ough | af ford' | clothes | castle |

23

| fudge | butter | oblige | ledge |
| grudge | gutter | obliging | pledge |

straight   birthday   swear
straighten   divide   won't

In which pairs was the second word formed from the first? Was any change made in the shorter words in these cases?

24. SPECIAL LESSON

On page iv of the Appendix you will find a list of holidays. Which are legal in your state? Learn to spell any which you have not already had, and review them all.

25. REVIEW

Review Lessons 16–24.

26

| drug | drug'gist | dis ease' | mea'sles |

croup   drawer   brake
knot   bicycle   tire

In what words does the combination *ea* occur? In which word does *ou* sound like *oo*?

Sixth Grade

27

"Haste makes waste."
Have you read "Madam How and Lady Why"?

| Mad'am | hinge | lounge | wrestle |
| glis'ten | piano | wither | squirm |

The quotation marks are used in the second sentence because "Madam How and Lady Why" is the title of a book.

28

garment	satin	calico	gingham
linen	travel	banana	
quarrel	molasses	cocoa	

How many words in this lesson are the names of materials? Which word ends in *in*? in *en*? Which have silent letters?

29

dance with ease	for your sake	meet a bear
sing a duet	a greasy plate	fresh beets
grease	sirup	ginger
greas'y	really	drowned

30

tas'sel	lock'et	jack'et	jew'el ry
brace'let	lining	plunge	
frighten	notice	ruin	

Sixth Grade

31

tor′rid   tim′id   vain   stub′born
  ma rine′   satchel   parrot
  squeeze   address   offer

Which word in this lesson means *pertaining to the sea?* *burning* or *parching? obstinate? having a high opinion of one's self? wanting in courage?*

32

Change the verbs ending in *y* to the forms in *ed* and *ing* in this way: *satisfy, satisfied, satisfying.*

envy   supply   occupy   reply
  spread   envelope   kettle
  swarm   pattern   kindlings

33

The conductor tried to prevent the collision.

con duc′tor   ac′ci dent   ex plode′   sense
col li′sion   re sult′   common   bowl

34

Mortar is made by mixing lime, sand, and water.

sieve   varnish   painful   raisins
strength   trouble   gentleman   coffee

  Spell *sieve* and *mortar* aloud five times.

Sixth Grade

35. REVIEW

Review Lessons 26–34.

36

" Early to bed and early to rise,
　Makes a man healthy, wealthy, and wise."

| wealth | prov′erb | nature | library |
| wealth′y | scarce | cotton | laundry |

37

| owe | charge | payment | settlement |

ex pense′　　　furnish　　　stable
ex pen′sive　　watermelon　 vegetable

In what way are the first six words of this lesson related?

38

full of briers　　　sharp thorns　　　dining room
pleasant excursion　try to meddle　　all right

moose　　　tailor　　　janitor　　　master

39. DICTIONARY LESSON

With the help of your teacher, select five hard words from your reading lesson, and consult your dictionary for their pronunciation and meaning. Write from memory any of these words you are certain you can spell.

Sixth Grade

40

almanac   hurricane   messenger   message
  minister   geography   grocer
  history   arithmetic   bushel, bu.

Separate the first five words into their syllables and place the accent. Consult your dictionary to see if you are right.

41

For what is each of the following used?

starch   sponge   grid'dle   sep'a ra tor
  screw   arrow   postal
  wigwam   target   reserve

42

The horizon is the line where earth and sky seem to meet.

ho ri'zon   a're a   fright   language
hor i zon'tal   growth   sailor   example

What word changes its syllables and accent when adding a syllable? Which word has a silent letter? Which is like *light?*

43. SPECIAL LESSON

Review page iv of the Appendix. Give special attention to all abbreviations.

Sixth Grade

44

"Labor conquers all things."
"It is better to be trusted than to be loved."

| la′bor | trust | charm | reply |
| con′quer | re ward′ | injure | pity |

What word ends in *or*? in *er*? Spell *conquer* aloud five times.

45

Review Lessons 36–44. Give special attention to the words that you have missed. Study these from your notebook. Remember that the first step in studying a review lesson is to separate the words you need to study from those you are certain you can spell.

46

| deaf and dumb | less than usual | blue eyes |
| bale of cotton | the main avenue | isn't here |

| jerk | hoeing | dangerous | sailor |
| ankle | shoulder | forehead | explain |

47

pier	an′chor	route	en gi neer′
berth	navy	canary
vessel	tripping	voice

Which of the above words have to do with travel by water? Does the *i* or the *e* come first in *pier*?

Sixth Grade

48

The garden has a border of geraniums.

| bor′der | gar′ret | a gree′a ble | quail |
| ge ra′ni um | ex press′ | ostrich | enough |

49

| mat | grit | tan′gle | business |
| mat′ting | grit′ty | tack′le | customer |

What is a *prefix*? A letter or syllable added to the end of a word is called a *suffix*. What change was made in *mat* and *grit* before adding a suffix? Review the *ing* forms of *put, run, hop, drop, set*.

50

The scent of roses and of lilies was in the air.
Is the peony a fragrant flower?

| pe′o ny | o′dor | giant | postage |
| fra′grant | loop | losing | parcel |

Look out for the pronunciation of *peony*.

51

Change these adjectives to the forms in *er* and *est* in this way: *easy, easier, easiest*. Add *ly* to *heavy* and *pretty*.

| early | heavy | homely | pretty |

Sixth Grade

52

The policeman arrested the chauffeur for speeding.

| po lice′ | chauf feur′ | oriole | elevator |
| po lice′man | ar rest′ | swallow | razor |

Consult your dictionary for the correct pronunciation of *chauffeur*.

53. SPECIAL LESSON

On page vii of the Appendix you will find geography words. Review all that you have already learned, and with the help of your teacher select and learn any others you sometimes need to write.

54

What words in this lesson may be used in speaking of persons?

| maid | dunce | dwarf | mi′ser |

    mer′cy   reins   recite
    rifle   poetry   towel

55. REVIEW

Review Lessons 46–54.

56

barren soil   mountain peak   don't know
stupid error   good location   couldn't see

    guess   repeat   preacher
    price   erect   beginning

Sixth Grade

57

Our principal taught us to salute the flag.
The flag is sometimes called "Old Glory."

| glo′ry | prin′ci pal | ad mire′ | kernel |
| glo′ri ous | sa lute′ | loyal | choice |

58

| hus′tle | stum′ble | trem′ble | stran′gle |

| twin′kle | beaten | discover |
| giggle | examine | juice |

In what way are the first six words in this lesson alike? What sound does the *n* in *strangle* have? See how your dictionary marks the *n*. Use in a sentence each word in the upper row.

59. DICTIONARY LESSON

Have a rapid dictionary drill. Ask your teacher to dictate words, and notice how many you can find in five minutes. Then find the pronunciation of five words selected from your reader.

60

| aim | in quire′ | mis spell′ | wan′der |

| re sem′ble | holiday | located |
| sugar | present | commence |

Find the word that means *to spell wrongly; to be like or similar to; to point or direct at; to ramble; to ask.*

Sixth Grade

61

Did you ever play croquet?
The florist made a large bouquet of roses.

flo'rist   dec'o rate   cro quet'   parade
taking   dec o ra'tions   bou quet'   chores

Consult your dictionary for the pronunciation of *bouquet*. In what way is it like *croquet*? Spell these words aloud five times.

62

occupation   preparation   separation   recitation
quotation   decoration   station

In what way are the words in this lesson alike? Separate them into syllables and place the accent. Mark the blunder spot in *preparation* and *separation*.

63

play croquet   troop of scouts   narrow margin
hit the stake   tiled bathroom   next Tuesday

turkey   whistle   erase
cranberries   merry   level

64. SPECIAL LESSON

On page vi of the Appendix you will find arithmetic words. Review any you have had, and with the help of your teacher select five others to study. Be sure to select words which you sometimes need to write.

Sixth Grade

65. REVIEW

Review Lessons 56–64.

66

Write a heading for this letter before studying the lesson.

Dear Mary,
  Mother and I return to the city next week, and we hope that you will accept our invitation to make us a visit. I am sure that you will enjoy Boston. Please do not disappoint us.

Your affectionate friend,
Helen

Separate into their syllables all words having more than two.

67

The magazine article was altogether too long.

mag a zine′	al to geth′er	flame	solid
ar′ti cle	fu′el	alarm	wonderful

How many *l*'s are there in *altogether*? Look out for *article*.

68

breast	court	livery	limit
reckon	throat	blood	
wrist	troop	cedar	

Use in a sentence each word in the upper row.

Sixth Grade

69

The nozzle of the hose is apt to leak.
I cannot imagine what the trouble is.

| im ag′ine | flowed | besides | cheat |
| noz′zle | angry | stranger | already |

70

| possible | favorable | usual | probable |
| possibly | favorably | usually | probably |

Separate all the words into their syllables. Tell clearly how the second word of each pair was formed from the first.

71

| au′thor | mer′chant | may′or | a′gent |

serv′ant   shadow   neighbor
blossom   passenger   hatchet

Which words can be used in speaking of persons? Which words end in *or*? in *ant*?

72

knead   Did you ever knead bread dough?
knight   A true knight always protected the weak.

| chal′lenge | thresh | husband |
| dis grace′ | spangled | daughter |

What other words beginning with silent *k* have you learned?

Sixth Grade

73

Tobacco was sometimes used for money in Virginia.

| loan | to bac'co | parent | among |
| cu'ri ous | com'merce | wife | toward |

74

lunch eon   spin ach   cloves   ci der

growth   above   prevent
against   crooked   hedge

Place the accent where it is omitted. Draw a line under the blunder spot of each word.

75. REVIEW

Review Lessons 66–74.

76

grant a request   a slight cough   will soon heal
wreath of holly   study hygiene   sure enough

hy'gi ene   fierce   pleasant   height

77

chap'el   ga rage'   cap'i tol   bun'ga low
ken'nel   balloon   interest
blizzard   fortune   daily

For what is each building named in the upper row used? Do not confuse *capitol* with *capital*. What does each mean?

Sixth Grade

78. DICTIONARY LESSON

Pronounce the following words very distinctly and spell each aloud. Close your spellers and spell the words from memory. Consult your dictionary to see if both spelling and pronunciation were correct.

peony   bouquet   chauffeur   automobile
garage   bungalow   spinach

79

"No home is too small for two friends, or too large for two enemies."

enemy   coun'ty   brain   hoarse
enemies   col'o ny   nostril   sprinkle

80

continue   introduce   introduction   manufacture
article   wrinkle   exchange
nickel   purse   gather

Separate the first five words into their syllables and place the accent. Use each in a sentence.

81

china vase   rural free delivery, R. F. D.
loaded dray   sixth-grade course of study
touch   hollow   instead
farther   radiator   motion

Sixth Grade

82. SPECIAL LESSON

Review the numbers and all the abbreviations you have had on page v of the Appendix. Give special attention to the last column of the first section of number words.

83

" He's armed without that's innocent within."
We lived in comfort on the special train.

| in'no cent | coax | leaped | homely |
| spe'cial | live'ly | evil | awful |

84

flea	heif'er	mos qui'to	mosquitoes
	hello	sewer	echo
	remember	drain	signal

There are several troublesome words in this lesson. Find and underline all the blunder spots.

85. REVIEW

Review Lessons 76–84.

86

A man full of *power* is said to be *powerful*. Note how *full* is spelled in these derived words.

| faithful | successful | truthful | powerful |
| peaceful | skillful | hopeful | graceful |

[255]

Sixth Grade

87

" He who refuses to remedy a wrong is guilty of a second wrong."

| re fuse′ | man′age | guil′ty | scribble |
| rem′e dy | man′ag er | drizzle | wrench |

What silent letter is there in *guilty*? What does *remedy* mean?

88

mo′tor	motorman	motorcycle	gas′o line
	punc′ture	bicycle	automobile
	tire	brake	chauffeur

89

complete failure	grizzly bear	pare an apple
repair my shoes	storm of sleet	lose a nickel
fearful	camel desert	several

What words contain *ai*? What word contains *el*? *ete*? Use each phrase in a sentence.

90

Review Lessons 86–89, and also the following words. When *ie* and *ei* have the sound of long *e*, which form usually follows the letter *c*?

| pier | receive | thief | priest |
| niece | believe | deceive | ceiling |

[256]

Sixth Grade

MID-YEAR REVIEW

91. REVIEW

Review Lesson 3, page 235, and Lesson 4, page 236.

92. REVIEW

Review pages ii and iii of the Appendix.

93. REVIEW

Be sure to make a list of the words you need to study, and cross out each word as it is mastered. It will be mastered when you can spell it orally or write it without hesitation.

absence	china	delivery	gingham
accept	cider	difference	glisten
accident	cistern	disease	glorious
affectionate	collision	disgrace	grease
agent	comfort	dishonest	guilty
almanac	complete	earnest	handsome
altogether	conductor	engineer	hinge
article	conquer	excursion	horizon
attempt	contain	expensive	hurricane
author	continue	failure	hygiene
border	court	favorably	imagine
bouquet	croquet	flavor	increase
breast	curious	fuel	innocent
challenge	currant	garage	inquire
charge	cushion	gasoline	introduce
chauffeur	decorate	geranium	invitation

Sixth Grade

94. REVIEW

jewelry	odor	repair	stupid
linen	omit	request	successful
livery	patience	resemble	supply
located	peony	return	syllable
lovable	police	rinse	thorough
luncheon	possible	route	threat
magazine	possibly	rural	thrown
manage	power	salad	tiled
manufacture	preparation	salute	timed
margin	principal	satisfy	tobacco
mayor	probably	scarce	torrid
merchant	produce	scenery	tremble
mercy	propose	scout	truant
message	puncture	separator	twinkle
mosquito	purpose	servant	usual
motor	quality	sieve	usually
nostril	quotation	special	wander
nozzle	receive	spinach	wealth
obedient	recitation	sponge	woolly
occupy	remedy	stubborn	wreath

95. SPELLING MATCH

Have a spelling match, using the words reviewed in Lessons 91–94.

Sixth Grade

96
The shepherd will shear his sheep.

shep'herd	treat	errand	cities
wea'ry	speech	canoe	dessert

What difference in spelling is there between *sheep* and the first syllable of *shepherd*?

97

sur'face	en'trance	mu'ci lage	gram'mar
al'pha bet	coconut		exact
beefsteak	prunes		temper

What vowel do you find in the last syllable of each word in the upper row? Spell these words aloud many times.

98

"Every right action and true thought sets the seal of its beauty on person and face."

ac'tion	so'ber	fancy	prize
beau'ty	stead'y	royal	saucy

99

deep	broad	wide	long
depth	breadth	width	length
high	ail	first	
height	trail	thirst	

Sixth Grade

100

An isle is a small island.

isle	moist	chan'nel	simple
aisle	mois'ture	pro vi'sions	legal

Isle and *aisle* are pronounced alike. How does the spelling differ? What does *aisle* mean?

101

undertake	themselves	newspaper	reindeer
however	fireproof	harrow	
chisel	southern	screen	

What words contain two shorter words?

102

piece of tape	barbed wire	yoke of oxen
bargain sale	bamboo furniture	leap aboard
awl	debt	value	straight
trowel	account	valuable	smooth

There are many useful review words in this lesson. Study only those you have forgotten how to spell.

103

pro'gram	or'ches tra	so pra'no	so'lo
al'to	square	cabin	
severe	sleeves	alley	

Sixth Grade

104
Does a cyclone or a blizzard do more damage?

| cy'clone | freak | earth'quake | officer |
| dam'age | i'ci cle | butcher | plumber |

105. REVIEW

Review Lessons 96–104, and also the following contractions. Tell for what each stands.

| isn't | howe'er | wouldn't | he's |
| o'er | doesn't | that's | we'll |

106

| unusual | impatient | unable | unpleasant |

    judge   ghost   arrange
    dentist   honest   noble

What prefix has each word in the upper row? How does the prefix change the meaning of the simple word? Does the use of the prefixes *un* and *im* make the words harder to spell?

107

| cinnamon bun | first aid | sore heel |
| future success | athletic sports | quire of paper |

| amuse | advance | preserve | accuse |

Copy the hardest words, and underline the blunder spot in each. Spell the words aloud as you copy them.

Sixth Grade

108

General Gibbs and Captain Powers were in full uniform.

Both officers have excellent records.

General, Gen.	ex′cel lent	re spect′
Captain, Capt.	rec′ord	copper

109. SPECIAL LESSON

With your teacher's help, make a list of the industries and manufactures of your city. If you live in the country, make a similar list for your state. Copy the words into your notebook and learn to spell them. Be sure to review these words as well as those in your spelling-book lessons.

110

saw and plane	private property	wring clothes
original poetry	profit and loss	sew a seam
iron metal	parlor	furnace

Time yourself to see how long it takes you to learn this lesson. Your lesson must be perfect if you wish a record for your speed.

111

du′ty	tab′let	ci′pher	sphere
ac′cu rate	mistake	liquid	
season	idle	separate	

In which words does *ph* have the sound of *f*? Consult your dictionary if you find an unfamiliar word.

Sixth Grade

112

"Knowledge is power."
The time of the auction is not yet known.

| knowl'edge | pan'el | mixture | trough |
| auc'tion | riv'et | traveler | stomach |

Knowledge is often misspelled.   Mark the blunder spot.

113

de feat'	cul'ti vate	en'ter	com pare'
de sign'	heart	dough
knuckle	couple	concert

114

"Attention is the mother of memory."

| reasonable | moan | orphan | coward |
| protection | groan | heroes | mercy |

Copy all the words having more than one syllable. Draw a line between the syllables and place the accent.

115. REVIEW

Review Lessons 106–114, and review also any words you have had in the arithmetic list on page vi of the Appendix. This is not too long a lesson if you waste no time on words you know. As a matter of interest, see how many words you can spell aloud correctly in one minute. Ten minutes of hard, steady study is enough for a very long review lesson.

[263]

Sixth Grade

116

Do not grieve over what cannot be helped.

grieve	ad vice′	wor′ry	primary
grief	ti′dy	worried	exercise

Does the *e* or the *i* come first in *grief* and *grieve*?

117

di gest′	re cov′er	ap′pe tite	nour′ish ing
im prove′ment		lonely	freight
eraser		scorch	wharf

Use in a sentence each word in the first row.

118. DICTIONARY LESSON

Have a dictionary speed contest. See how many words dictated by your teacher you can find in five minutes. For the remainder of the lesson look up the pronunciation and meaning of five words selected by your teacher from your reading lesson. When all the words have been found, pronounce each one very distinctly three times. Can you spell any of them simply from looking at them?

119

yolk of an egg		regular train	ought to go
a beautiful scene		stanza of poetry	wrap up
yolk	harbor	curtain	furniture
folks	whittle	cellar	bureau

Sixth Grade

120

"United we stand, divided we fall."

| fact | pre′cious | mirror | which |
| fa′ble | afterwards | faucet | separate |

Look up *precious* in the dictionary for exact meaning and pronunciation.

121

rot′ten	dif′fi cult	ter′ri ble	wick′ed
bash′ful	guide	healthy	
brought	breathe	column	

Find the word that means *horrible; shy; decayed; hard to do; evil in practice,* or *sinful.*

122

The yacht was a total wreck.

| to′tal | squall | question | basement |
| shal′low | figures | merrily | piazza |

123

al′co hol	anx′ious	cer′tain	ruf′fle
ce′re al	surprise	handkerchief	
doughnut	parasol	feather	

What other words that you have had end like *certain?* Try to make a list of at least four.

[265]

Sixth Grade

124

The building has granite foundations.
A large quantity of stone was required.

| fudge | saucer | beneath | rather |
| yesterday | measure | below | mighty |

125. REVIEW

Review Lessons 116–124, and also all geography words you have had in the list on page vii of the Appendix. Do not forget the notebook words. Keep a record of the time it takes you to learn this lesson. If you do not fail on any words, put the date and the time into your notebook and see if you steadily gain in the future.

126

dominoes   vinegar   refrigerator   funeral
   kerosene   medicine   automobile

Separate into their syllables all the words in the first row. Place the accent and consult your dictionary to see if you are right.

127

Wanted. Boy to make himself useful in a grocery store after school hours. Good position for a strong, honest boy. Boy owning bicycle preferred.

T. B. Jones, 85 Main Street

| pre fer' | po si'tion | ad'ver tise |
| pre ferred' | forgotten | ad ver'tise ment |

Sixth Grade

128

stare arrive pause inclose

 chosen bandage reduce
 cement welcome practice

Change the verbs in the first line to the forms in *ed* and *ing*.

129

Brass is formed by the union of copper and zinc.

group per form' search dispute
in clude' improve prepare uniform

Look out for *union*. What word would you have if the *u* were changed to *o*?

130

cottage factory palace theater

 tenement scout badge
 trolley hospital basin

What words are the names of buildings? For what is each used? Separate *theater* into syllables and place the accent.

131

civil answer gypsy camp eight cents
opposite house the proper way forty dollars

pity ferry sausage poison
pitied island perfume jewel

Sixth Grade

132

clev′er	in struct′	sparrow
ar′gue	legal	robin
space	drawn	oriole

Use in sentences the words *legal*, *space*, and *drawn*. Spell the *ed* and the *ing* forms of *argue*, consulting your dictionary if you are in doubt.

133

A country ruled by an emperor is called an empire. Our country is a republic.

na′tion	savage	mutton
na′tion al	reason	bakery

What vowel changes its sound when *nation* becomes *national*?

134

admission	permission	possession	explosion
	expression	journey	district
	mischief	generous	injury

In what way are the first five words alike? Separate them into their syllables and place the accent.

135. REVIEW

Review Lessons 126-134 and also your notebook words. Keep a record of the time it takes you to learn this lesson perfectly.

Sixth Grade

136

The refreshments consisted of cake and vanilla ice cream.

Henry is more industrious than his cousin.

| in'dus try | lightning | tomorrow |
| in dus'tri ous | bristle | caterpillar |

137

wa'ges   pur'chase   re ceipt'   sam'ple

part'ner   tying   neither

walnut   lemonade   because

Does the *e* or the *i* come first in *receipt*? What letter preceded the *e*? In what other words does the *e* come first after *c*?

138

do a favor   familiar music   national hymn

a short reign   safety first   baseball team

joke   insect   surely   evening

What word ends in *or*? Where is the blunder spot in *familiar*?

139. DICTIONARY LESSON

Here are a few words you have had which are often mispronounced: *perfume, peony, automobile, national.* Look up the pronunciation of each and repeat each distinctly three times. Remember that the accent will help you. Have a five-minute drill in finding words rapidly.

Sixth Grade

140

explanation   describe   description   certainly
generally   machine   buffalo
deserve   obliging   beetle

Separate all the words into syllables. If you pronounce each syllable, you will not omit it when you write.

141

"Nothing venture, nothing have."

ven′ture   false   dis turb′   distance
dis tinct′   falsehood   further   although

142

How many verbs in this lesson end in a single consonant after a single vowel? Which syllable of these words is accented? Change them to the forms in *ed* and *ing* in this way: *permit, permitted, permitting.* What change was made besides adding the suffix?

per mit′   o mit′   ad mit′   oc cur′
control   priest   chorus   extra

143

dye   They will dye the satin red.
dyed   The women dyed a piece of coarse cloth.
dyeing   They are now dyeing some linen.

Do not confuse *dying* and *dyeing*. Use the first in a sentence.

Sixth Grade

144

flee   capsize   combine   decide
frown   president   mineral
nephew   prisoner   products

What word means *to unite*? *to run away*? *to scowl*? *to overturn*? *to settle* or *conclude*?

145. REVIEW

Review Lessons 136–144, and also the following words:

tongue   stomach   choir   separate
whether   receive   believe   Wednesday

146

Do you object to my attending the concert?
No, I have no objection whatever.

ob ject′   at tend′   re mark′
ob jec′tion   re port′   collection

Pronounce *object′* distinctly. What does the word mean when it is accented in this way: *ob′ject*?

147

graceful creature   direct route   ripe olives
model kitchen   settled region   capital letter

examination   jealous   capture
dictionary   appear   pebble

Use each phrase in a sentence.

Sixth Grade

148

| guest | stu′dent | mu si′cian | um′pire |

    rel′a tive   doubtful   bruise
    size   collect   direction

  Which words in this lesson may be used in speaking of persons? Use each in a sentence.

149

    The entire troop was attacked and surrounded.
    They were finally fortunate enough to escape.

fi′nal   diamond   review
fi′nal ly   sparkle   natural

150

engage   engagement   employ   employment
    idleness   replied   worst
    rising   negroes   hoping

  In which words are the suffixes *ment* and *ness* used? Was any change made in the simpler words before adding the suffix?

151

Your sincere friend   Your affectionate son
Sincerely your friend   Affectionately yours
Truly your friend   Yours respectfully

  Which form would you use in a letter applying for work?

Sixth Grade

152

" Make yourself necessary to somebody."

| nec′es sa ry | pe′ri od | plat′form | wagon |
| pro mo′tion | prog′ress | custard | courage |

What letter in the first syllable of *necessary* has the sound of *s*? Pronounce the word very distinctly and spell it aloud as you copy it.

153

| mischief | liquor | photograph | patient |
| mischievous | destroy | notch | secret |

success   agree   safely

Separate these words into syllables and place the accent. Which word changed a letter before adding a suffix?

154

| telephone receiver | call " Central " | too early |
| telegraph wire | receive a telegram | sow seed |

artist   source   trousers   succeed

In which words does *ph* sound like *f*? What other words have you learned in which this occurs?

155. REVIEW

Review Lessons 146–154, and also these words:

| scissors | clothing | dessert | desert |
| bureau | search | practice | surprise |

Sixth Grade

156

| de ceit′ | hope | neglect | hate |
| de ceit′ful | re venge′ | peace | thought |

To which of these words can you add the suffix *less*? To which can you add *ful*? You have learned to drop the final silent *e* before the suffixes *ed* and *ing*, both of which begin with vowels. Consult your dictionary to see if final *e* is dropped before *less* and *ful*, which begin with consonants.

157. SPECIAL LESSON

With the help of your teacher make a list of the principal rivers of your state, the lakes, if any, and the railroads in your part of the state. Copy the names into your notebook and learn to spell them.

158

The athletic contest drew a large audience.
It was an important event in the neighborhood.

| con′test | im por′tant | people |
| au′di ence | neigh′bor hood | oyster |

159

baggage	machinery	violin	revolver
mattress	gentle	distant
soldier	avenue	except

Separate the first four words into syllables. Use each in a sentence.

[274]

Sixth Grade

160
What is your favorite style of dress?

| styl'ish | fash'ion | pigeon | cream |
| ma te'ri al | chocolate | whipped | actor |

There are some hard review words in this lesson. Study the ones you are not sure you can spell.

161

pardon	relieve	shudder	instruct
suspect	innocent	shield	
measles	manager	straighten	

What word means *to tremble with fear or cold?* *to forgive?* *to mistrust?* *to free from a burden or from distress?* *to teach?*

162

Honor and justice go hand in hand.
My opinion of her gradually changed.

| disappoint | livery | heifer |
| motorcycle | limit | alphabet |

163

sa'cred	psalm	re li'gion	ser'mon
beauty	breathe	cyclone	
action	bamboo	excellent	

What letters in *psalm* are silent?

Sixth Grade

164

Words of opposite meanings:

| birth | native | sense | depth |
| death | foreign | nonsense | height |

| light | strong | honest | coward |
| heavy | weak | dishonest | hero |

165. REVIEW

Review Lessons 156–164 and the following words:

believe	receive	pier	grief
grieve	priest	niece	ceiling
deceitful	thief	deceive	piece

166

| elevated railroad | twentieth century | el′e vat ed |
| electric cars | won the contest | e lec′tric |

| e lec tric′i ty | king′dom | beggar |
| cen′tu ry | ghost | ashamed |

How many syllables are there in *electricity*? Be sure to pronounce them all.

167

graze	re joice′	ex plore′	pro nounce′
re move′	deaf	scent
expense	dumb	florist

Change the verbs in the first row to the forms in *ed* and *ing*.

Sixth Grade

168

They threw their influence on the right side.
They also urged and encouraged others to do so.

in'flu enceim'i tatewealthy
en cour'ageim i ta'tionmessenger

169

cozysplendidcunningnervous
numerouswomanparlor
thiefsunsetattempts

Make phrases by joining an adjective with a noun in this way: *cozy parlor*.

170

It is an honor to entertain the governor.

gov'erngov'ern mentshearathletic
gov'ern orentertainmentcinnamonproperty

What two words end in *or*? Be sure to pronounce the *r* in *govern, governor,* and *government*.

171

pierceselectretreatlaunch
unitedigestgranite
spheredifficultposition

Find the word that means *to withdraw* or *to retire*; *to join*; *to cause to slide into the water*; *to choose*; *to thrust into* or *to bore*.

Sixth Grade

172

No difficulty seems too great to one who is determined to succeed.

sensible	courageous	pause
determined	horrible	print

Copy the words having more than one syllable, and spell them aloud as you write. Place the accents. Consult your dictionary to see if you are right.

173

correction	murder	whiskers	married
wedding	nation	industrious	
argue	falsehood	graceful	

What change is made in *marry* before adding *ed*?

174

broken axle	innocent victim	rapid writer
dangerous adventure	famous battle	of course

dan'ger ous	fa'mous	possibly	receiver
ad ven'ture	rap'id	mayor	violin

175. REVIEW

Review Lessons 166–174 and all words in your notebook that were selected with the aid of your teacher. See how many words you can spell aloud in a minute, taking them just as they happen to come, long or short.

Sixth Grade

176. REVIEW

Review Lesson 3, page 235, and Lesson 4, page 236.

177. REVIEW

Review Lesson 93, page 257, and Lesson 94, page 258.

178. REVIEW

Use each homonym in a sentence, to show its meaning:

| need | made | night | sent |
| knead | maid | knight | scent |

| birth | capital | flea | coarse |
| berth | capitol | flee | course |

accurate	beauty	duty	favorite
action	central	dyeing	foreign
admission	century	electric	fortunate
advertise	cereal	encourage	foundation
advice	certain	entertain	future
alcohol	cottage	entrance	general
alphabet	creature	excellent	governor

anxious	cultivate	explanation	grammar
appetite	damage	explosion	grieve
arrive	deceitful	factory	guest
attention	decide	false	honor
audience	describe	familiar	horrible
baggage	destroy	famous	icicle
bargain	disturb	fashion	imitation

[279]

Sixth Grade

179. REVIEW

important	neighborhood	rapid	soprano
improvement	nervous	receipt	steady
industry	nourishing	refrigerator	student
influence	occur	region	style
justice	opinion	regular	surface
kerosene	opposite	reign	telegraph
knowledge	orchestra	relative	telephone
liquor	original	relieve	terrible
machinery	pardon	religion	theater
material	permission	republic	total
memory	photograph	respect	union
mischievous	pierce	revenge	venture
moisture	possession	safety	vinegar
mucilage	precious	scene	weary
musician	prefer	select	width
national	private	sensible	worry
necessary	psalm	shepherd	wreck
neglect	quantity	sincere	zinc

180. SPELLING MATCH

Have a spelling match, using the words reviewed in Lessons 176, 177, 178, and 179.

APPENDIX

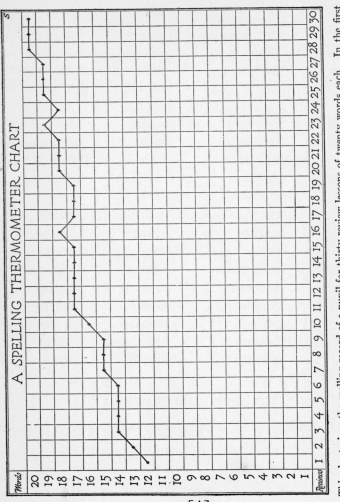

This chart gives the spelling record of a pupil for thirty review lessons of twenty words each. In the first review the pupil spelled twelve of the twenty words correctly. He put a dot in the middle of the square in the first row that is opposite the figure 12. In the next lesson he spelled thirteen words correctly, and therefore put a dot in the middle of the square in the second row that is opposite the figure 13. He then drew a straight line between the two dots. The record for the remaining reviews was kept in the same way.

Appendix

WORDS OFTEN MISSPELLED

The following common words have been found to be among the most troublesome in our language. The first list contains one hundred and forty words frequently misspelled, and the second (on page iii) contains a number of homonyms which are often wrongly used.

able	break	cousin	February
ache	built	daily	forty
afraid	buried	deceive	friend
again	business	different	gone
against	busy	divide	grease
almost	button	doctor	guess
already	buy	does	guide
always	can't	dollar	half
among	careful	done	having
angel	center	don't	heard
answer	chief	double	height
any	choose	dying	hoarse
beautiful	clothes	early	hoping
because	collar	easy	hour
been	color	either	instead
beginning	coming	enough	juicy
believe	cough	every	just
blue	could	farther	knew
bought	country	father	know

Appendix

laid	once	since	wear
lesson	piece	some	weather
library	pleasant	straight	Wednesday
loose	please	sugar	where
lose	quiet	sure	whether
lying	quite	tear	which
making	raise	they	whole
many	read	though	whose
meant	ready	tired	woman
minute	receive	tonight	women
much	said	trouble	wonder
neither	says	truly	won't
ninety	seems	Tuesday	would
ninth	separate	until	write
none	shoes	used	writing
often	should	very	wrote

Homonyms are words that are pronounced alike, but differ in spelling and meaning. The following homonyms are often wrongly used. Use each in a sentence.

here	week	there	meet	great
hear	weak	their	meat	grate
its	dear	threw	to, too	pear, pare
it's	deer	through	two	pair

[iii]

Appendix

Sunday, Sun.   Monday, Mon.   Tuesday, Tues.
  Wednesday, Wed.   Friday, Fri.
  Thursday, Th.   Saturday, Sat.

January, Jan.   May   September, Sept.
February, Feb.   June   October, Oct.
March, Mar.   July   November, Nov.
April, Apr.   August, Aug. December, Dec.

LEGAL HOLIDAYS AND SPECIAL DAYS

Labor Day   Lincoln's Birthday
Hallowe'en   Saint (St.) Valentine's Day
Thanksgiving Day   Washington's Birthday
Christmas Day   Arbor Day
New Year's Day   Memorial Day
  Fourth of July or Independence Day

ABBREVIATIONS OF WEIGHTS AND MEASURES

inch, in.   pint, pt.   peck, pk.   day, d.
foot, ft.   quart, qt.   bushel, bu.   week, w.
yard, yd.   gallon, gal.   ounce, oz.   month, mo.
mile, m.   dozen, doz.   pound, lb.   year, yr.

Appendix

ABBREVIATIONS

Mister, Mr.
Mistress, Mrs.
Miss

Doctor, Dr.
Captain, Capt.
General, Gen.

Street, St.
Avenue, Ave.
Number, No.

forenoon, A.M.
Post Office, P. O.

afternoon, P.M.
Rural Free Delivery, R. F. D.

railroad, R. R.

NUMBERS

one	nine	seventeen	sixty
two	ten	eighteen	seventy
three	eleven	nineteen	eighty
four	twelve	twenty	ninety
five	thirteen	twenty-one	hundred
six	fourteen	thirty	thousand
seven	fifteen	forty	million
eight	sixteen	fifty	zero

first	fifth	ninth	thirteenth
second	sixth	tenth	twentieth
third	seventh	eleventh	once
fourth	eighth	twelfth	twice

one half   hundredth   thousandth

Appendix

SPECIAL LISTS
ARITHMETIC

addition	subtraction	multiplication	division
add	subtract	multiply	divide
plus	minuend	multiplicand	dividend
amount	subtrahend	multiplier	divisible
prove	remainder	product	divisor
proof	difference	partial	quotient
fraction	simple	percentage	problem
proper	complex	per cent	cancellation
improper	compound	rate	square
numerator	factor	profit	cubic
denominator	terms	discount	ratio
reduce	decimal	insurance	proportion

GRAMMAR

subject	clause	singular	antecedent
predicate	phrase	plural	gender
declarative	noun	nominative	masculine
interrogative	proper	possessive	feminine
exclamatory	collective	objective	neuter
imperative	verb	present	analyze
adjective	transitive	future	adverb
comparison	intransitive	participle	adverbial
positive	active	pronoun	preposition
comparative	passive	personal	conjunction
superlative	tense	relative	interjection

Appendix

MARKS OF PUNCTUATION

comma ,	semicolon ;	quotation marks " "
period .	hyphen -	interrogation mark ?
colon :	apostrophe '	exclamation point !

GEOGRAPHY

Eastern Hemisphere	North America	Europe
Western Hemisphere	South America	Asia
United States	Australia	Africa

Atlantic	ocean	continent	mountain
Pacific	strait	island	valley
Arctic	river	peninsula	plain
Antarctic	bay	isthmus	plateau
Indian	gulf	cape	prairie

volcano	population	commerce	transportation
desert	products	domestic	latitude
oasis	minerals	foreign	longitude
area	mining	exports	parallel
surface	agriculture	imports	meridian

zone	frigid	tropical
torrid	equator	axis
temperate	tropics	revolve

Appendix

DIACRITICAL MARKS

There are twenty-six letters in the English alphabet, but there are many more sounds. Some letters, therefore, must serve for several different sounds, and the diacritical marks are used to show which sound a letter has in a given case. The marks here given are those used in the Webster's New International Dictionary.

A few diacritical marks have special names, as those used with the following words:

cāne, macron; měn, breve; wõrk, tilde; câre, circumflex; reçeive, cedilla.

Vowel Sounds

ā as in cane	ê as in there	ū as in cube
ă as in mat	ī as in mine	ŭ as in tub
ä as in arm	ĭ as in tin	ũ as in turn
a̗ as in fall	i̇ as in firm	u̗ as in full
â as in care	ĩ as in machine	ṳ as in rude
ȧ as in ask	ō as in hope	ȳ as in try
a̤ as in was	ŏ as in hot	y̆ as in truly
ē as in be	õ as in work	ỹ as in myrtle
ĕ as in met	ô as in for	o͞o as in cool
ẽ as in her	o̗ as in tomb	o͝o as in look

Consonant Sounds

Most consonants have but a single sound, and in these cases no diacritical marks are necessary. The following consonants are not marked when they have their most common sounds:

ç as in receive	ġ as in engine	s̩ as in has
çh as in machine	n̩ as in wink	t̶h as in this
¢h as in chorus	x̣ as in exact	